# Fear Not; God Is in Charge

## Pastor Florence Maina

Copyright © 2019 Pastor Florence Maina.

All rights reserved. No part of this book may be used or reproduced by any means, graphic, electronic, or mechanical, including photocopying, recording, taping or by any information storage retrieval system without the written permission of the author except in the case of brief quotations embodied in critical articles and reviews.

WestBow Press books may be ordered through booksellers or by contacting:

WestBow Press
A Division of Thomas Nelson & Zondervan
1663 Liberty Drive
Bloomington, IN 47403
www.westbowpress.com
1 (866) 928-1240

Because of the dynamic nature of the Internet, any web addresses or links contained in this book may have changed since publication and may no longer be valid. The views expressed in this work are solely those of the author and do not necessarily reflect the views of the publisher, and the publisher hereby disclaims any responsibility for them.

Any people depicted in stock imagery provided by Getty Images are models, and such images are being used for illustrative purposes only. Certain stock imagery © Getty Images.

ISBN: 978-1-9736-5344-8 (sc)
ISBN: 978-1-9736-5345-5 (e)

Library of Congress Control Number: 2019901722

Print information available on the last page.

WestBow Press rev. date: 08/28/2019

# Acknowledgement:

I am forever grateful to God, my maker, my all in all for putting ideas about this book and the grace He bestowed upon me to bring it to completion after very many years. Amen!!

To my entire family – My husband Charles, my children, Moses, Esther and David, my sweet grandchildren, Liam, Grace and Mercy. You were all very patient and understanding as I spent many hours and days working on this book. You are the best family God gave me. What you could have regarded as negligence, you regarded it as investment. You are all very precious to me!!

Erin Heyduk for being an encouragement and spending many hours in the library trying to help me organize and spell check the original manuscript. It was tough, really tough but it was not in vain.

Betsy Bohan, Writer, Speaker & Registered Nurse - for your writing expertise insights and encouragement.

Pastor Dave Reno, former lead Pastor of Grace Fellowship, my home church. Your encouragement and prayers after I shared what I was working on was very fruitful.

Dishon W. Wambugu, Kenya for your continuous encouragement despite the distance as you consistently kept telling me, I have the potential to do it. Finally, it's here!!

Wayne Corrigan, Global Missions Coordinator, Grace Fellowship, MN – Giving me a listening ear as I shared many times my burden of service with you. Your encouragement and even taking time to witness my ordination were all stepping stones to bring this book to the final step though you had no idea.

My mentors: Dr. Charles Karuku, CEO and founder of ILM and senior pastor of IOC & Pastor Zipporah Bogonko, Minnesota, USA.

My fellow Twin Cities pastors and those who relocated to other states just to mention a few: - Michael Ngeru K. (KCOC, St. Paul), Peter Kamore (Destiny Hill, Minnetonka, Laura and Sam Githinji (JCC, Twin Cities), Emily Lagat (Inspired Prayer Ministries Int.), Risley Prakism, (New Life Church, St. Paul, MN), Daniel Bosire (DFM, Brooklyn Park), Munene Mwangi and Steve Ibabu, Seattle, Washington

My first pastor when I landed USA, Dr. Rev. Jin S. Kim, senior Pastor Church of All Nations, Columbia Heights, Minnesota, USA. Like in the time of Elijah, you are in my time frame of this journey of "Fear Not, God is In Charge" book.

My ministry colleagues: IGS and CYMWJ teams, Minnesota Women Prayer Team, Minnesota Kigoco Organizing Team. The Lord brought you all in to my life with a divine assignment. Even without knowing the details of my life, you individually made calls and continue to do so just to check on me or wanting to visit me or to provide for a financial need. God bless you because behind the scene, most of those calls came when I was at the verge of giving up on this book and your words of encouragement and prayers without knowing bounced me back to action. Here it is now!!

My Kenyan community leaders: Samuel Mwangi, Executive Director/ Founder Global Fatherhood Foundation, Joan Misoi, Total Care Assisted Living, Josephine Mbiti-Nyanoti, Carol Kuria of Kenyan

Youth Initiative, MN. Thank you all for your continued encouragement in my service for God and the people He brings in my life. You have been my behind the scene spiritual pillars like Moses, Aaron & Hur were to Joshua and the team in the battlefield as well narrated in Exodus 17. Your individual inputs in my life have been like single pieces of a Puzzle that can never be complete if one piece is missing.

Tim & Christine Ko, California, USA

Erik & Barbara Olson, Plymouth, Minnesota, USA

Tom & Joan Lee, St. Paul, MN, USA

Maxine Pierson, RN, EHN, Presbyterian Homes, MN, USA

Phillip & Andrea Lee, Plymouth, MN, USA

Bishop Rgt. Rev. Stephen G. Njenga, Seattle Washington, USA

Pastor John Cordova, Care Ministry, Grace Fellowship, Brooklyn Park, MN

To you, reader of this book which I believe will be a blessing and you will be a blessing to someone else as you share the insights and encouragement you will derive from it.

# Contents

Preface . . . . . . . . . . . . . . . . . . . . . . . . . . . . . . . . . . . . . . . . . . . xi
Chapter 1   Fear and Its Causes . . . . . . . . . . . . . . . . . . . . . . . . . 1
Chapter 2   Why We Should Never Fear as Christians . . . . . . . . . 9
Chapter 3   Whatever Your Status, Fear Not . . . . . . . . . . . . . . . . 25
Chapter 4   Fear Not as You Give . . . . . . . . . . . . . . . . . . . . . . . . 50
Chapter 5   You and I Are Pilgrims on Earth . . . . . . . . . . . . . . . . 72
Chapter 6   What the Bible Says about Fear . . . . . . . . . . . . . . . . 83
Chapter 7   Fear Not if You Trust the Lord . . . . . . . . . . . . . . . . . 100
Chapter 8   Why Some People Fear and Others Don't . . . . . . . . 118
Chapter 9   Overcoming Inner Fear . . . . . . . . . . . . . . . . . . . . . . 137
Chapter 10  The Best Way to Deal with Fear . . . . . . . . . . . . . . . 159

# Preface

THE WORLD TODAY is faced with fears of all kinds. Every person expresses fear of some kind, and there seems to be no human solution, because as the days pass, more fears come. Students fear what to do after their education is over due to the large population and lack of jobs due to economical strains. Parents fear for their adolescent children when they become unruly and don't heed any of their advice; the influence of peer groups contradicts their expectations. Young people fear sharing their hearts with parents since they think they will be ignored or misunderstood; instead they end up looking for help from the wrong sources, which, instead of solving the problem, create more fear. So what next?

Even mature children still bother their parents with fear as they combat evil ways, such as immorality, drug addiction, and so forth. Nations fear the increased crimes day by day, and every effort to overcome this situation seems to open more doors for more serious and dangerous crimes than before.

In the medical circle, doctors fear the increased number of unknown and undiscovered diseases as they endeavor to find ways to manage already-existing diseases. There are shortages of medicines. This problem increases fears because though they want to assist in eradicating diseases, the shortage of medicine continues as the consumption increases. Also, while one medicine helps a particular problem, another medicine is created because of the side effect of the previous one, and fear continues. The chain of fear in the universe increases every day.

In the agricultural circle, farmers worry about the many increased and unknown harmful insects, which mess up the crops before their management is known. Harmful weeds such as the hyacinth, which has startled scientists due to its quick spread and cover over certain lakes, have led to the scarcity of fish. In the same field, seasons are no longer as predictable as they once were, when every farmer prepared farms for the expected rains for a particular season. These days rain comes as a surprise to most of us, and hence there is the fear of losing more seedlings in the ground due to a lack of rain and then never yielding anything.

In marriages, there are so many fears, and some spouses can never fully trust their spouses. Why? This problem is due to infidelity, divorce, in-laws' threats, inheritances, the lack of children, and so forth.

It is for all these reasons that I felt persuaded to write this book. I share with readers what has encouraged me the most due to my meeting people of different backgrounds with diverse fears in my daily life either at work, school, home, in church and even as I travel for mission work to different places as chances allows. I have been privileged to travel to several parts of the world on missionary work like in Europe, India, the United States, and many parts in my motherland Kenya. Therefore, at least I have a bit of knowledge about the fears people face.

Pastor Florence Maina

# Chapter 1

# Fear and Its Causes

FEAR CAN CAUSE anxiety, which can affect our health. But the light of God is there to help us overcome fear.

Once, I was preparing to sit for an examination, and I had some fears. I was afraid of the questions I would be expected to answer in that particular test; I feared that maybe I hadn't studied the course materials enough. If a student hasn't studied the syllabus fully, fear is obvious. And so to me, failure to meet some established rules and regulations can easily cause fear.

A cost is mandatory to studying; sometimes you must overlook your social life and fun to get good grades. In this pursuit, one must realize and accept that such denials are worth it all for the future benefits. Sleeping fewer hours than expected to study for that test is worth it if you can earn a good grade—even though it's not comfortable when you sacrifice that sweet sleep (especially during a cold winter). Getting out of your comfort zone is never easy, but for focused achievement, you choose with all wisdom as you expect something positive in return no matter the cost. That is preparation worth all the denial, and in the end, it brings forth more additional benefits, such as scholarships based on performance, enrollment in honor societies (which gives added advantages when it comes to placement in colleges), and good-paying jobs with little manual work.

An expectant mother can fear the outcome of her baby's health if she neglects to attend the prenatal care appointments regularly and scheduled routine checkups. Observing healthy eating habits, getting extra sleep to relax for the sake of the unborn, and reading necessary materials all call for self-discipline, but they are also necessary for a healthy bouncing baby. Good preparation means fewer doctors' visits, meaning fewer call-in times and days which brings good production at work places.

A soldier on the battlefield can easily fret if he or she fails to have access to the entire armory as expected. Obedience to the initial expectations from the commander will only make a soldier happy when commissioned to the field for battle. You and I are soldiers in the army of the Lord, and our commander, Jesus, expects us to put on the whole armor of God in obedience to give us victory in our day-to-day living as we face various challenges on the spiritual battlefield. I have had different experiences regarding being prepared and not prepared or equipped. Since the flesh is always weak, whenever I am tempted to act without spiritual armor, I end up with regrets and tears of repentance. However, when I am equipped and prepared, I experience peace and joy both in myself and in the other party concerned. Always being ready is another factor that contributes to victory, since once we are summoned, we don't get mixed up in the preparation process.

This journey calls us always to be ready because our opponent, the devil, is roaring like a lion, eagerly looking for someone he can devour. Being ready when he comes won't threaten us at all, but we will just do the needed fighting. Jesus gave a parable of the ten virgins to show how vital preparation is. All the virgins had lamps, but not all took the extra initiative of putting oil in them, which might not have been a requirement at the time.

We have no time to waste on the battlefield, since we are on full and serious business. How ready are you if the enemy confronts you now? Get ready, because he is coming, even if he hasn't come before. Oh, what a privilege we have, because the armor is ready for us to put on. If you are in civilian clothes, take them off and put on this armor as referenced in Ephesians 6.

## Fear Not; God Is in Charge

A farmer who hasn't tilled the land in good time always dreads hearing a drip of rain. Why? He is caught unprepared. Are you ready like that farmer who works in good time and must be ready to plant once the rain comes? Hard work is required to avoid fretting. Lazybones always has a good reason to dread, because he or she fails to comprehend where to start once the rain pours heavily. When prepared, you have a reason to be grateful and even encourage others to be ready too. And in waiting, you will be busy fulfilling other responsibilities, for there is always something to do in families, churches, offices, schools, orphanages, hospitals, and food banks; you can also mentor and guide people who are lost in this generation and seem to learn better through technologies and media that sometimes can be very misleading. When you pray for them, you name them all. Do you think there is nothing else for you to do? Look for volunteer opportunities all around you.

Personally, I do several volunteer works in different places: - through work, I knew there was more for me than just getting a pay check at the end of every pay period. Since March, 2013 I have been involved with SafeJourney program through my work. It is a 24- our service free of charge offered through men and women who give in their time to be present for victims of domestic abuse. As part of the team, all I do is sign up for two shifts monthly and I have experienced what God can do once there is a willing vessel to be used for someone who is hurting. Look around you what you can do!! Visit your home page community services section and see what areas you can be a blessing to someone who can never pay you back!!

In the spiritual realm, you have a land to till your heart. You must work hard on your salvation once you accept the Lord, which is only the first and not the final step. No wonder Paul clearly warned the Philippians, "Wherefore, my beloved as ye have always obeyed, not as in my presence only, but how much more in my absence, work out your own salvation with fear and trembling" (Philippians 2:12KJV). Our God is hardworking, and we have nobody to blame if all we want to do is sit and wait for miracles to fall on us from heaven.

Praying persistently by faith is work; reading God's word, sharing the gospel, and actively serving in your local church require hard work. But this work has good fruits, among which will be your spiritual growth and stability. This work can also open doors for your call to serve in specific areas that otherwise couldn't have been a reality if you had just remained dormant. In the kingdom of God, nobody has been called to be a spectator; rather, we are all called to participate. How long have you been a spectator? It's never too late to change. Rise up and take your position in the kingdom- not as a slave but as a coheir with Christ, the King of glory.

As a believer, you've got something to bring to the kingdom of God, and He who calls is faithful and won't let you down. Are you afraid others won't appreciate you? Be assured that the Lord recognizes every single thing you do for His glory, no matter how little or small - you name it. Our work in Him isn't in vain, and all records are clear and well kept in place for the day of remembrance. They are uplifting, just like they were with Mordecai as well recorded in the book of Esther. At the appointed time, Mordecai's good work was rewarded. (Reference Esther 2)

Sometimes we go through situations that make us in our humanity think there is no hope. But glory to God who intervenes and starts afresh with us when we speculate we are all done. Do you remember such times? God is in charge of all records, and you won't be forgotten forever. Take heart. Redeemer, the holy one of Israel is in charge and will delegate your package of favor. Get ready to sing praises to the Lord, for He is about to assign the angels to bring you to your elevated level.

I would rather be appreciated and remembered by God than by people, because once He says, "Well done," others have to say it too. Amen. When Jesus says yes, no person can say no; when He lifts you up, nobody can put you down; when He blesses you, no one can say otherwise; and when He promotes you, nobody can demote you. Be encouraged and embark, working for God without reservation. Serve God with all your strength, not only some, because He gives you everything you have. And above all, you aren't your own; you belong to Him, so give glory to His holy name.

## Fear Not; God Is in Charge

Even when you work and prosper, it is He who gives you that strength to be rich—and without Him, you are and have nothing. When we reach that comprehension, we can totally surrender all to Him despite the challenges that will always be there anyway. We are His children, and as a Father, He always has our best at heart. He provides the best package in life that suits our needs (not our wants); this provision is a huge thing for us as human beings.

As a parent, I understand this better because a seven-year-old son will ask for a car but in reality want a toy. Who as a caring, loving parent with full sense would fulfill that request? Do you get the point now? Often when we approach God in our prayer closet, we ask many things, some of which we never realize are only wants and not needs. As a loving heavenly Father, He will obviously meet the needs and leave out the wants. We feel offended, since as children we don't distinguish between these two until we learn something later when all has been fulfilled.

Glory to God who will always make sure at some point that we come back to ourselves and remember why He never gave us what we initially asked for. At that point, our hearts rejoice and start worshipping Him in awe of His majesty. Therefore, fear not when all you have been praying for hasn't been answered your way. He has your back covered and won't let you be dismayed. Fear not! Again, He is telling you not to fear, no matter what you are going through. Do you feel like you are done with God? He isn't done with you yet; He is just starting on your business, and you will be amazed by who He is and what He will do for His name's sake.

Before our family migrated from Africa, we went through tough times with financial strains, and we lost most of our friends, but God stood with us. When my husband received the report of the green card acceptance, which he had applied for earlier to come to America, no man could deny the hand of God at work. When God remembers you, He makes all the difference, and He ends all the sorrows of your forgotten moments by friends or relatives. Our morning dawned as the psalmist said (Psalm 30:5). God was in charge, and in His calendar; our month of breakthrough from financial suffering was culminating.

Obeying God's word only when we are in the company of fellow Christians but not on an individual basis wherever we are isn't enough. We are called on to be faithful servants always, whether our colleagues see us or not; otherwise if we walk righteously in only favorable circumstances, then we are no better than the Pharisees, whom Christ always referred to as hypocrites. In season and out of season is our call that God commands. This way, *fearing* will be a word that doesn't find a place in our lives.

How is your life, my friend? Do you always fear? Check on your obedience to the laid-down rules and regulations of your respective surroundings and work on them, and you will be a winner who encourages others not to fear because the Lord expects us to live fearlessly in Him.

Another cause of fear in life is the way our Christian lives appear before God. We are expected under all circumstances to live smooth lives that are well pleasing to our maker. If you walked with a true friend, you would do introductions in case you met someone you knew who didn't happen to know your friend. What do you think your friend would feel if you failed to introduce him or her? What answer do you have?

One day as I was going to work, I noticed from where I took *matatu* (public transportation) to the office that there were so many potholes. Every time a vehicle came from the other side of the road, it endeavored to escape the potholes, which were at the center or side of the road but at different places. On this particular day, I happened to witness this problem with several vehicles; all seemed to escape the potholes and preferred the smooth part of the road.

At this juncture, God quickened my spirit, and a revelation came to me. When we have sins in our lives, they act like potholes in our spiritual lives. God isn't able to bless us as much as He would want to because sins hinder His presence in us. As He comes with blessings, desiring to pour them on us, a spiritual pothole makes it hard for Him. Isaiah 59:2 says, "But your iniquities have separated between you and your God, and your sins have hid his face from you that he will not hear."

## Fear Not; God Is in Charge

In the same way, as was revealed to the prophet Isaiah, we find that sins become stumbling blocks in our lives and that no blessings can come; hence, we are left with no option but to fear every day because we face different challenges. Potholes in our Kenyan roads have been known to cause the many accidents that have claimed many of our citizens and left others crippled throughout their lives. As one vehicle driver tries to avoid a pothole, he or she collides with another vehicle coming from the opposite direction, thus causing an accident.

Spiritual potholes have caused accidents, which have claimed many Christians, leaving some backslidden (dead spiritually) and others crippled in such a way that they aren't able to face a sinner and testify that Jesus Christ is Lord. At other times, they fail to read the word of God, which is our light. They find the satisfaction of Sunday services, but there are no prayers as Christ used to pray, yet He is the Son of God. There is no intercession for the nation, yet the word requires us to intercede why is this? Because spiritual potholes have been entertained instead of covering them with the word of God, prayers, fellowships, and the preaching of the gospel of the Lord Jesus Christ.

It's surprising when you see a certain Christian passing through a place where the gospel is being preached in the company of unbelievers. Confidently, he or she passes without even speaking a word of encouragement to the people he or she is walking with (while being ashamed of the gospel). The reason is that there are potholes in his or her life. May God help us confidently say with Paul, who was never ashamed of the gospel, "For I am not ashamed of the gospel of Christ; it is the power of God unto salvation to every one that believeth to the Jew first and also to the Greek" (Romans 1:16). Unless the blood of Jesus Christ covers such potholes, many spiritual accidents will happen, and they will claim and cripple many Christians.

Be alert to spiritual potholes. In the storehouse of our heavenly Father, there are enough materials to cover our spiritual roads, unlike our earthly roads, when we have to wait until funds are available.

The blood of Jesus Christ is ever available to us anytime we order it in prayer.

As our spiritual road remains smooth without potholes, we shall surely say like Paul, "I have fought a good fight, I have finished my course, I have kept the faith" (2 Timothy 4:7). This is a sign of spiritual maturity that will easily eliminate fear. In reality, children are obviously afraid if left alone, and so are our spiritual lives if we do things on our own without the help of our heavenly Father.

Fighting a good fight requires preparations ahead of time. Daily spiritual preparation through prayers, reading God's word, and continuous service is a way of preparation that obviously equips us for battle, which we are bound to face every day. It's clear from scripture that the devil roars like a lion, looking for someone to attack, and that is you and me as believers; therefore, we see our need for daily equipping. This journey is an action that takes practice and requires us to be action-taking people while still redeeming the time because the days are evil. May God help us to avoid procrastination? Seize the moment because wasted time is like spilled milk, which can never be collected.

# Chapter 2

# Why We Should Never Fear as Christians

A GOOD REASON we shouldn't fear is because God has enough provision for each day we face. The Bible has enough provision for us every day to avoid giving in to fear of any type. All we need to do is ensure that we read it thoroughly. There are more than 365 (or 366 if it's leap year) "fear not"s in the Bible. Therefore, there is always a "fear not" each day for each person, irrespective of his or her race, status, and so forth from God, the Creator of heaven and earth. Every morning before we wake up, God has already given us a "fear not tablet" to use for the whole day's worries and strains. So in whatever we go through in our daily lives, we should be confident that there is a "fear not" from God specifically for you and me. Did you know that?

Be assured that our daily fears are always taken care of on the condition that we trust the Lord in all our undertakings. Nevertheless, we know that once we consult a doctor, he usually gives us medicine for treatment, but we have the ability and choice to do the rest. The doctor's last step is giving us the medicine, without which your situation cannot improve in any way until we take it. God's work is our medicine, and His last action to us is giving us the word. We have a crucial role of taking the word into our hearts by faith, without which we can never recover from our spiritual ailments, which are the root causes of the physical ones. Obeying the doctor's instructions and taking the doses prescribed are the keys to our recovery, and in the same way, our only medication through the word is the key to our daily victory in this journey. Therefore, we are the determining factor to our spiritual victory by depending on the word of God as required.

The Israelites feared when they were amid problems. In Exodus 14, the Red Sea was before them, and the chariots of Pharaoh were coming after them from behind. Realistically they had every reason to fret, but we should see things as Christians beyond the realities of every matter in the spiritual realm, because God will always intervene in His supernatural power and ways if we look unto Him and seek Him for whatever we undergo in life. The Israelites were helpless, and to walk with the Lord, we must be helpless and rely on His help, which is always good for us.

After all, if we get help when we don't really need it, we cannot value it as much. The many obstacles in life make us easily fear as human beings, and God expects us to turn to Him for help. By our own strength, we cannot overcome fear until we involve God and ask Him to assist us. The more helpless we are, the more we are bound to appreciate and share God's divine intervention and without doubt share His deliverance with others. At this point, in whatever challenges or problems you are going through, rejoice because when God stretches out His hand on your behalf, even those who may not believe in God's power will surely testify and say there is a God who can deliver and provide victory. And this will fulfill the scripture in Romans 8:28 {paraphrased} "All things work together for good to those who love the Lord and called according to His purpose." Notice this says *all things* not *some things*.

In this case, the Israelites murmured against Moses and complained about being taken from Egypt; they would have preferred to be back there than to experience their current trial. I always wonder why they hadn't complained at the beginning of the journey from Egypt. Nevertheless, it's a human weakness to start complaining when an

## Fear Not; God Is in Charge

obstacle comes. Life was well with them at the beginning, because they could foresee deliverance from their oppressive Egyptian masters.

Challenges in life today make many forget their initial call and purpose because human nature always likes seeing quick and easy-gotten victories. All the same, we should keenly note that easily attained victory is more cheaply valued than hard-gotten victory, which is more precious and handled carefully. If you recall, when you got saved, you were excited then, but on the path of life you started regretting when difficulties that were only temporal arose. In the same way, the Israelites in this case were no different.

Once, a Christian organization volunteered to sponsor people for a gospel trip to our African countries. All those involved were excited as they prepared, but a time came with problems when all of them started blaming the sponsors, whom they had been happy with in the beginning. Why? A problem came up, and the journey failed at the eleventh hour; it was beyond what they could have prevented. Prior to the unexpected failure, every person had joyfully testified of God's confirmation about the mission. The same people turned out to be enemies of the sponsors, and I failed to comprehend how and why, yet they were prayer warriors according to their testimonies. Just like the Israelites who complained to Moses, they complained to their good sponsors.

Unaccomplished agendas and missions easily bring fear, but as Christians, we should be careful to seek God to know His will and teachings from such occurrences. because *all* things, not *some*, work for good to those who love the Lord. Do you love the Lord? Then know that whatever comes to you, good or bad, is all for your good because you love the Lord. Whatever is good in that situation may be so good that in the long run, you will start regretting why you were complaining about it. Our God is such a good teacher, who glorifies Himself both in positive and negative circumstances. What a mighty God we serve!

Moses, instead of arguing with them, just encouraged them, "Fear not, stand still and see the salvation of the Lord, which He will show to you today; for the Egyptians whom ye have seen today, ye shall see them again no more forever, the Lord shall fight for you, and ye shall hold your peace" (Exodus 14: 13–14). They had to take an action of holding on to their peace to see the hand of God delivering them. God will never work in our anxiety, but when we hold our peace and trust Him, we always witness His divine intervention in our favor, but we have to be patient. Patience pays in the Lord because we can never wait on the Lord in vain. Our humanity likes to see things happening immediately when we request something from God, but in the same way, God may want to build character in you for His glory and even for the benefit of others in the future.

It's sometimes hard to encourage someone in a particular problem if you've not experienced it yourself; as the saying goes, experience is the best teacher. Keep on holding unto the Lord and His everlasting promises because He is always true. Unlike us human beings. It's always with a good reason that our God delays something when we pray. In most cases, He senses we can boast, and we regard ourselves better or more righteous than others if our answer comes very quickly after prayers. Be assured that all things are working out for your good because you are the called one of the Lord. So long as you are right before Him, take heart and let patience have its way in your life.

A thousand years is like a day before God, and a day is like a thousand years. What an encouraging statement that requires our patience! No institution on earth has an answer to this equation, but God has it right because His isn't man—glory to His holy and righteous name (1,000=1 and 1=1,000). Don't even try to google this equation since you cannot get it.

Moses here acted like a real servant of God and a leader too. In most cases you find that if such a situation occurred in our time, the most probable action to such complaints, as was in Moses's case, would be for the leader to blast off the people or just give up on them and continue as he reasons out that we should each carry our respective burdens. There is a time to carry your own burden and carry the burden of others, and this is still biblical. We need to be sensitive to the particular times we are in. When the Spirit of God

## Fear Not; God Is in Charge

leads us, we will be able to know our season of bearing the burdens of others and ours respectively.

We need to be spiritually alert to differentiate these times. Are you alert or just living? Wake up and be watchful lest you enter the trap of the enemy. This spiritual sensitivity will call for one who is strong in the Lord, not just human strength, because our battle is spiritual, not physical.

Moses was strong in the Lord; therefore, he was able to share his strength with the Israelites, and they were able to see, experience, and even witness the power of almighty God, which was beyond the reality. It is in such cases that Brother Paul urges every believer as he urged the Ephesians, "Finally, my brethren, be strong in the Lord and in the power of His might" (Ephesians 6:10). Strength in the Lord and of the Lord will always change hard situations, circumstances for the glory of His holy name.

Are you amid problems today? Do you wish you hadn't trusted the Lord in that situation like the Israelites? Take heart and see beyond the reality of your hard situation. Stand still and see the deliverance of the Lord, and you will be an encouragement to somebody later, who might be in the same hassle as you. Hold your peace and look to God, and He will deliver you.

God isn't a man that He should lie, neither a son of man that He should repent. Therefore, stand still, and He will see you through. Has He not said, "I will never leave you nor forsake you"? Jeremiah feared that he couldn't speak because he was a child, but the Lord encouraged him: "But the Lord said unto me, say not I am a child for thou shalt go to all that I shall send thee thou shalt speak. Be not afraid of their faces: for I am with thee to deliver thee saith the Lord" (Jeremiah 1:7–8).

In the previous verses, we see God telling Jeremiah, "Before I formed thee in the belly I knew thee: and before thou comest forth out of the womb I sanctified thee and I ordained thee a prophet unto the nations" (v. 5). Jeremiah's concerns were already cared for a long time before his birth. Many times we behave like Jeremiah and fear what God has already taken care of, even before we start fretting because we are today's Jeremiahs as Christians, the called ones of the Lord. He was mindful of his state, "being a child," yet God had ordained him before birth.

We can overcome fear only when we confidently know God is in control of every situation, be it bad or good, and that before we encounter it, He obviously prepared it to come specifically to us. Somebody shared and said that nothing comes to us through the backs of God's eyes. He weighs and sees that you or I am capable of going through it victoriously through Christ, who strengthens us. For sure I consent with this because I can look back at all that has ever come to me, good or bad. Though at the beginning of it I tend to see that it's hard and not allowed by God, when the victory comes, I always see myself as a fool before God. This has taught me to confidently believe that the harder the situation, the greater and sweeter the victory. At the very beginning, it may call for much crying and even swelling of our eyes, but personally I have many times experienced that the end of a hard beginning is far more encouraging than the beginning. A very dark beginning many times brightens up at the end, but the cost is normally met.

The way to know this is by living in the word of God, arguing in the word of God, and believing and obeying the word. Trusting and obeying are the principal truths for attaining victory in God. The word should be our compass for our entire lives, and just as a pilot cannot starts off without a compass, so should we desire to have the word of God for guidance in life. David the king was learned and widely traveled, yet he knew that being a king without the word of God was all vanity. Therefore, he said, "The word is a lamp unto my feet, and a light unto my path" (Psalm 119:105).

When it is dark, we use a lamp or flashlight to have light in the house. The life we live is full of darkness, and we cannot see a thing unless we use the word of God to be a lamp or a flashlight; therefore, we have the light for guidance to where we are heading. Without a compass, an airplane will always lose direction in spite of being piloted by someone who has all the needed qualifications. So will a Christian without the word lose the heavenly direction in spite of his or her status in the church or the many years he or she has lived in Christianity. What matters is the daily guidance of the word and not any achievements we have on earth. The word is the only benefit we have for our spiritual walk with God.

In a very dark house at night, you cannot see a thing, and you may fall as you endeavor to grasp something you are in need of. You may stagger into a closed bedroom door because you cannot see in the darkness. Can you clearly see how we stagger helplessly without the word of God for every situation? Yet it is there for our asking or request. Start now by taking a step of having it dwell richly in you, and you will notice the difference for your own good and for the glory of God.

In sickness there is a phrase, "By His stripes we are healed." "But He was wounded for our transgressions, he was bruised for our iniquities, the chastisement of our peace, were upon Him: and with His stripes we are healed" (Isaiah 53:5). Are you sick? Christ was wounded for your transgressions. The thirty-nine strokes He received were intended to deliver you from every infirmity that could be messing up your health.

Fear not because healing is the food of the righteous. It's the will of God that you be healthy so you will serve Him effectively. Receive your healing now by faith. Refuse all the convictions of your feelings and receive healing by faith. Testify after you are healed to glorify your redeemer, Jehovah Rapha. Let your healthy body now be active in the work of God as you tell others of His love toward all sickness, which Christ delivered you from two thousand years ago. Fear not because God is a merciful God in sorrows. "Surely He hath born our grief, and carried our sorrows: yet we did esteem Him stricken, smitten of God and afflicted" (Isaiah 53:4). You have no reason to be sorrowful because Christ did it for you. Resist the enemy, who always rejoices to see you sorrowful. Imagine Christ carrying your sorrows on His shoulders. That is good news, and being burdened with a load someone has volunteered to assist you with is mere foolishness. You see how we ignorantly carry unnecessary burdens, which aren't ours as the children of God. Fear not now that you know that the joy of the Lord is your strength. Make the devil inert by claiming the power of Jesus, which is your right and not a privilege if you are a child of God.

The battle isn't ours but the Lord's, who will fight for us, and every weapon fashioned against the righteous will never prosper. The Lord encouraged Jehoshaphat when he was in fear, and He reminded him that the battle was His. "Thus saith the Lord unto you, Be not afraid nor dismayed by reason of this great multitude; for the battle is not yours but God's" (2 Chronicles 20:15).

Looking to God for victory in battle requires our ignorance toward our physical surroundings. Multitudes who could be against you are no problem to God. The problem is always that you and I fail to take God at His word. Yes, weapons may be fashioned against you, but what does God promise in His word? Fear not because though they are fashioned already, they won't prosper. Amen. Your business isn't to worry about your foes, but yours is to hold on to the promises of God pertaining to battle. God is God, and He is true, and even if you doubt, He still remains true and faithful.

Many people in the Bible feared, and God encouraged them in their fears, so take heart because the word of God is at your asking as you read from Genesis to Revelation and other Christian literature written by men and women inspired by the Holy Spirit. During the time of battle with Goliath, the Philistine, David's brothers and the entire people of Israel dreaded to confront Goliath because of his might, but David courageously confronted him in the name of the Lord. In his own strength and might, he couldn't have managed, but he took the word of God and hence killed Goliath despite his might. That challenge in your life will be like Goliath, in total defeat if you take God at his word like David did.

What is that big threat you fear? Approach it in the name of the Lord by faith, and victory will be yours, and you will live to glorify God. David only took an action and you must, and God will intervene on your behalf. David by faith saw beyond the reality of Goliath's might, who was far much mightier compared to David, but he knew the God of Israel was mightier than any visible armies of Goliath.

## Fear Not; God Is in Charge

What is that big threat you fear? Approach it in the name of the Lord by faith, and victory will be yours, and you will live to glorify God. David only took an action, and you must, and God will intervene on your behalf.

"And there went out a champion out of the Philistines, named Goliath, of Gath, whose might was six cubits and a span. And he had a Helmet of brass upon his head, and he was armed with a coat of mail; and the weight of the coat was five thousand shekels of brass. And he had grieves of brass upon his legs, and a target of brass between his Shoulders. And the staff of his spear was like a weaver's beam; and his spear's head weighed six hundred shekels of iron: and one bearing a shield went before him" (1 Samuel 17:4–7). These four verses were written purposely to describe this champion of the Philistines, Goliath. Realistically he was mighty, and all fears the people had for him were normal, but spiritual things are completely not as we would argue normally, realistically, physically, emotionally and so forth. But spiritual things are spiritually designed, and they must be spiritually tackled. That challenge you are fretting about could be greater than that Goliath description, but take heart because that word of God you hold on to by faith will be more effective to conquer that same situation.

God purposely allows that challenge so you will experience His divine intervention and deliverance, which are beyond human expectations. Remind God of what He has promised because He must act at the mention of His word in prayers. Laziness and doubts are the only things that hinder spiritual breakthroughs in our day-to-day lives. Wake up and take your stand spiritually in Jesus's name. Victory will always be yours if you hold on to the peace of God and let Him fight the battle for you. Claiming His promises is giving Him your burden and reminding Him that on your own without Him, you are already a loser to the devil.

Putting on the *whole* armor of God is the key to your battle, and your victory is already guaranteed. This guarantee isn't temporal but forever. We are used to periodical guarantees of the accessories we normally buy, but our spiritual guarantee from God is forever.

Nothing is too hard with God, even that great challenge that seems laborious to you now.

"And David was the youngest: and the three eldest followed Saul. But David went and returned from Saul to feed his father's sheep at Bethlehem" (1 Samuel 17:14–15). What these people could see brought the fear. What are you seeing as an obstacle and hence bringing fear in your life? Look to God, the maker of all in the universe, and you won't fear. What we see with our eyes removes our spiritual eyes from God and paralyzes our faith, which is the hand of receiving anything from God combined with prayers.

Why worry when you can pray in faith? Don't allow the devil to threaten you by bringing an obstacle to prevent your heavenly journey. Let him know you are a child of God, and you will run to report him with all those scary things he is threatening you with. When we pray, we report our foe to our mighty God, who will intervene for our deliverance. Contrary to Goliath's big and detailed description due to his physical strength, David was only a young shepherd. You may not have a big title or be qualified academically, but if you know you stand in God, you will be a winner despite the obstacles. David realistically couldn't even be allowed a chance to even try to fight Goliath, but because he knew his God, he was able to go beyond human expectations.

If you know your God, you can do exploits even today. As many rely on their earthly achievements, choose to rely on the Lord for victory in your daily life. David wasn't even in the program of going to fight with the champion, but his three older brothers, who were physically of good appearance in men's eyes, were in the program at least. Our age or whether men recognize us is immaterial to God; we see that David wasn't even close to being mentioned, since among the eight sons of Jesse, he was the youngest, and only the three eldest sons were taken to the battlefield. Even if there was a second chance of Jesse's sons, David still wouldn't have been among them since there were four more brothers between him and the first-chosen lot. God isn't a respecter of persons.

You and I may be very far in the programs of men, but if we are

## Fear Not; God Is in Charge

God's choice for His divine purpose, take heart. God will surely use us at the appointed time. What matters is what God says about you or plans for that matter. Many times we fail because we look at things with our physical eyes instead of our spiritual eyes of faith. Don't allow the devil to intimidate you by bringing an obstacle to prevent your heavenly journey. Let him know you are a child of God, and you will report him with all those scary things he is threatening you with when you pray. We report our foe to our mighty God, who intervenes for our deliverance.

David's brothers and all the Israelites feared Goliath's appearance because they saw only physically, discarding the faith element, which enables us to go beyond the normalities of life. A normal human being is expected to have five common senses, and missing one or having one more makes us regarded as abnormal in human eyes. Faith is the sixth common sense, and hence it should catalyze us to see and take things beyond the human perspective but always pleasing to God. If you are being regarded as a lunatic because you take God at his word, take heart because we had better obey God than man. We better rejoice over being approved by God rather than by men.

David was living his normal life of a shepherd when his chance of fighting the champion, Goliath, came; his father sent him to take food to his brothers in the battlefield. "And Jesse said unto David his son, take now for thy brethren an ephah to thy brethren; and carry these ten cheeses unto the captain of their thousand, and look how thy brethren fare and take their pledge" (1 Samuel 17:17–18).

It was in his lowly position that he found the chance of going to the battlefield as he performed his duty of a messenger. His father, Jesse, sent him as a messenger, and he obeyed. You could be only a messenger, but as you obey the way David obeyed his father as a boss, you may attain a chance of being used by the Lord, and you will be a wonder to the highly esteemed lot as they wonder how and why. Suppose David murmured when his father sent him; he could have gone with a heavy heart and couldn't have taken the challenge the way he took it there at the battlefield.

As we serve God, we need to have a cheerful heart, willing as we obey our earthly masters and bosses, knowing that it's through obeying that chances will arise for our service for God. We see here that David had no inferiority complex because if he had, he could have just taken food and quickly returned to his lowly duties, but now he appreciated his work. Many people don't do so in the world we are living in unless it's a white-color job, which is prestigious. From time immemorial, God has used the lowly in more crucial incidents than He used the royal lot, so you have no need to fret because of your low physical status, because your spiritual status will bring a change in your surroundings. Moses was looking at the flock of his father-in-law when the Lord appeared to him. Joseph was serving as a mere house boy in Potiphar's home when the chance came for God to use him. Mordecai was another one who was always at the gate while his opponent, Harman, was seriously recognized, but God still recognizes the less unfortunate according to human's judgment for His own glory. The list in the Bible of such people is long. Read and you won't undermine yourself under the influence of the enemy.

"And David left his carriage in the hand of the keeper of the carriage, and ran into the army, and came and saluted his brethren. And as he talked with them, behold, there came up the champion, the Philistine of Gath, Goliath by name, out of the armies of the Philistines, and spoke according to the same words: and David heard them. and all the men of Israel, when they saw the man, fled from him and were sore afraid" (1 Samuel 17:22–24). "And David heard them." These words enlighten my mind on the importance of being a keen listener. If we are to overcome fear in the spiritual way effectively, Christians need to be keen listeners as the Bible calls us ambassadors of Christ in this world. When you are keen, you will manage to man fear easily since even in very challenging situations, you will take all to God in prayer.

The devil has introduced another style of decency in Christianity for being organized. By this I mean if you are decent, you will use words as poking one's nose where not needed, attending issues on appointment's basis only. I thank God that in Christ, we don't always need to be so organized as to follow appointments when urgency arises for fighting fear. David wasn't supposed to hear what the Philistine champion, Goliath, was saying because it was none of his business, but as a shepherd, he was used to being attentive to safeguard the flock. His normal life was an advantage in this case.

What do you do for a living? Whatever your work is, you have a better chance to serve God. David was a shepherd who stood for God. As a messenger, you have a very good chance of giving the word where you run errands during your business. There is no time to waste. Start where you are. The devil has a good-invented syndrome to invest fear in the lives of others to prevent their crucial roles in the kingdom of God. This syndrome has chased many from the churches today who could be effective intercessors, evangelists, counselors, and so forth.

## Inferiority Complex Syndrome

Once this syndrome attacks, it becomes very hard for one to accept that he or she is in the perfect will and plan of God to fulfill His purposes on earth, especially in the body of Christ. This chronic syndrome makes one compare himself or herself with others of higher status, and hence, a bomb of "You aren't in the right company" goes off, rendering one powerless. Yet in the eyes of God, you could be more powerful spiritually than those you regard as better than yourself. God's ways aren't like those of people, who always look on the outside appearance and stability, but He looks on the heart. The hearts of those you could regard as better than you could be very far from God and filthy, hindering any breakthrough for God to use them in any way.

As lowly as you could be before men, you could be very precious in the sight of God if your heart is well with Him. In the entire Bible, you find that the lowly were always used more than highly esteemed people from a human perspective. The determining factor for God to use us is being available, willing, and holy, which is contrary to men's measure of use and credibility. Trusting and obeying God, combined with the prior mentioned, are all you need and not just seeing yourself as a grasshopper before your counterparts. Remember the Israelite leaders Joshua sent to spy out the land of Canaan; what they saw scared them to the extent of making them forget what God had promised them. Don't let those you fear prevent God's plan for you. You are well able if you are key in the eyes of God.

Be like Caleb as a servant of God. He fought fear and ignored the voices of his colleagues. He had another spirit that made him see beyond the visibility of human ability. Ignore your surrounding pressures, which are weighing down your spiritual stand in God. Look to God by faith. Didn't David ignore all the discouragement, mockery, and undermining of his elder brothers and trusted the Lord? The outcome of moving under the inspiration of the Holy Spirit gave him victory over the prior-feared Philistine, Goliath. Stand firm in God. He is a good refuge, a present help in times of need. Lean not on your own comprehension but release yourself fully to God and tell Him that you know that with Him, all will be well.

Jesus was another keen person. In many cases where He attended to people, as recorded many times in the Bible, He wasn't initially set for those particular missions, but He needed to interfere for the sake of their deliverance from the fear of different types.

John 4:3–7 says, "He left Judea, and departed again into Galilee and he must needs go through Samaria. Then cometh he to a city of Samaria, which is called Sychar, near to the parcel of ground that Jacob gave to his son Joseph. Now Jacob's well was there, Jesus therefore, being wearied with his journey, sat thus on the well: and it was about the sixth hour. There cometh a woman of Samaria to draw water: Jesus saith unto her give me to drink."

Jesus's appointed destiny was Galilee, although He passed through Samaria. It was a long journey, and He grew tired and therefore sat at the well of Jacob about the sixth hour. This clearly shows that were it not for His human character that grew tired, He wouldn't have sat at the well; and hence, no chance would have arisen for Him to meet this woman. His being tired, which many of us may not appreciate in our heavenly journey, created the chance for this woman's deliverance from her day-to-day fears in the society of her time. In the same way, some negative things come to us at one time or another; a chance may arise for our deliverance from fear, being taught of the Lord about

## Fear Not; God Is in Charge

spiritual maturity and so forth. "All things work together for good to them that love God, to them who are the called according to his purpose" (Romans 8:28).

So here we can see that Jesus's appointed destiny was interfered with, delayed by His tiredness, and the same brought deliverance to the Samaritan woman and many others, whom this woman went testifying to as she ran, saying, "Come and see a man who has told me all things…." (John 4:29 KJV).

May God help us to see things clearly and spiritually, and we shall always be a people full of praise, which overcomes threats of life, and thanksgiving, since we know that *all* and not *some* things works for good. Amen. Let us be ready to have our good, organized time disrupted for the glory of God, our appointments canceled or delayed so that something good, out of what we may term as negative, may be attained. It is when we live that way and believe the same that we will manage to say together with Paul, "In everything give thanks for this is the will of God in Christ Jesus is concerning Jesus you" (1 Thessalonians 5:1). In this same text, we see this Samaritan woman was also on her business of drawing water. "There cometh a woman of Samaria to draw water" (v. 7). While in her own important business, Jesus interrupted her, and I thank God that she didn't ignore Him. "Jesus saith unto her, Give me to drink" (v. 7). This woman's business never prevented her from listening to Jesus the way our businesses hinder many of us from listening to the master Jesus. Let not your business and commitments of this world prevent you from listening to the Savior because soon and very soon, you will leave those things you value most behind when Mr. Death visits you. Have your priorities right, and you won't have regrets. The kingdom of God is the key principle to good success. The woman's positive response brought deliverance to her entire life and others as she went shouting, "Come and see a man who has told me all things." We should also note that our listening to God will cause our deliverance for our entire lives, just the way this woman and others, whom we relate to, saw their lives changed by Christ.

Many words we easily hear in evangelism are "I am busy now.

Come another time. I have so many appointments today. Where are you from? Which denomination do you belong to?" All of these words show fear of being removed from your good religion, but we shouldn't fear being in the hands of the mighty God. As we go out to preach, we should never talk of our religion, but giving the gospel of the good news of peace is the acceptable principle. Religions never save people from fear but only bind them with rules and regulations, causing more fear instead of eradicating it. As I mentioned earlier, I have an evangelistic burden, and these are the questions I have always heard every time I am out on a mission, mostly in the door-to-door sessions. Frankly speaking, I consider all these questions as broken cisterns that cannot hold water because our being busy can't take us to heaven unless we are busy with the Lord and for the Lord. "Another time" is a phrase the devil uses to hook ignorant people. My friend, resist him now, accept the Lord to save you, and escape the hoodwinking of the devil, who will always let you have those words because he knows his time is short for humbugging the children of God. Many appointments in our lives cannot cancel the once-and-for-all appointment from God, <u>Mr. Death</u>. Once death comes, all other appointments are canceled forever without your choice, and after death comes judgment. Our backgrounds and nationalities are also immaterial before God, who calls all men to repentance. Our denomination isn't a passport to take us to heaven, but we have a passport from Jesus, because He is the Way, the Truth, and the Life. Amen. Look back, my friend, and remember the many times you have ignored the word of God through the public media, personal evangelism, and take a step.

You have been ignorant for too long. Ask God to forgive you, and because His mercies and loving kindness endure forever, He will deliver you like He did the Samaritan woman. Now go to a servant of God who is near you for prayers and embark on evangelism, of which you have been ignoring for too long. Be a vessel to let others do the right thing in this area. You can also buy copies of this book and send them to those you feel you cannot easily reach, and you will be blessed as you assist them in fighting fear.

## Chapter 3

# Whatever Your Status, Fear Not

NO MATTER YOUR status, learn to stand firm in God. He is a good refuge, a present help in times of needs. Lean not on your own comprehension but release yourself fully to God and tell Him you know that with Him, all will be well. The Bible has several records of the lowly people God used for very vital roles, and we can look at a few examples of such lowly people, whom we can learn a lot from, so the devil does not mislead us.

### Fisherman Whom Jesus Called: Simon and Andrew

"Now as he walked by the sea of Galilee, he saw Simon and Andrew casting a net into the sea: for they were fishers. And Jesus said unto them, Come ye after me, and I will make you to become fishers of men and straightway they *forsook* their nets, and followed him" (Mark 1:16–18, emphasis added). So long as you aren't lazy, your lowly status can be a very good chance to be used of God when you obey fearlessly.

### James and John

"And when he had gone a little further thence, he saw James the son of Zebedee and John his brother, who also were in the ship mending their nets. And straightway he called them: and *they left their father* Zebedee in the ship with the hired servants, and went after him" (Mark 1:19-20, emphasis added). In spite of them being fishermen, God saw in them a quality He could use to enlarge the kingdom of heaven. They were busy in the low status. I hope you also don't go idling because idleness and laziness are self-inflicted, bad characteristics that cannot be used for any benefit in the kingdom of God. Let not the enemy lure you about with empty convictions that being low means to have a low self-esteemed. No! You can be much more of use in the kingdom of God than those around you whom you fear just because of their earthly possessions, which are temporal. The biggest percentage of people who are rich in earthly possessions are the poorest people spiritually, and they are always fearful of their possessions' security.

The advantage of lowly people is that all they have is within their reach. I assure you, it's safer spiritually with less than with much. Jesus noted this when a certain ruler briskly confessed that he had obeyed all the commandments in the Law of Moses. When he was told to go and sell everything and distribute it to the poor, the ruler was reluctant because to him all those riches meant so much to him. He was very sorrowful because of worldly riches (Luke 18:18–23).

Are you attached to your worldly possessions to the extent of being sorrowful when the Lord needs you? Change your way of life if you expect to have any inheritance in heaven. "Seek ye first the kingdom of God and his righteousness" (Matthew 6:33). Set your priorities right, which determine your eternity. From these people, we note that they (1) forsook and (2) left their father. When they heard the Savior calling them, they obeyed without question like many of us do these days because of fretting about what the future will be when we hearken to the Savior's call. Our future is in the hands of God, and we should therefore eliminate worries by obeying the conviction of our consciences when God needs us. Our fearing the future only adds more problems because as human beings, we cannot know what the future holds. Our God, who is the same yesterday, today, and forever, knows what we are fearing. With all this knowledge, if I were you, I

## Fear Not; God Is in Charge

would do away with the frets of life ASAP and tell God, "Lord, take over my life and let it be consecrated to You from now henceforth." It's a wise decision because you will attain a source of comfort that does not dry up. Your fellow allies can only console you for a while but not forever. This can easily be comprehended by thinking of our dear ones, who normally lose their relatives and next of kin through death. In most cases friends manage to comfort them for only a period of time until the burial time. After that, most homesteads are normally deserted with only God to fill the vacuum of a valuable, lost dear one.

Now back to the sons of Zebedee; we clearly note that because of their immediate obedience, they were promoted from being fishers of fish to fishers of men. Jesus told them, "*I will make you become*" (emphasis added). Anytime Christ called people from time immemorial, He always made them become. *Become* is a very heavy word in the spiritual realm. It's being made to be something while you were nothing of any spiritual benefit. "But as many as received Him, to them gave the power to *become* the sons of God, even to them that believe on his name" (John 1:12, emphasis added). From this verse, you can note that before receiving Jesus, they weren't sons, but afterward, they were sons.

Do you want to become a child of God? Then meet the condition first of accepting Christ, the Son of God, and you will become one. Don't be satisfied where you are because there is a missing factor to make you become one. That missing factor is Jesus. These people forsook what they needed most for a living, since fishing was their job, just because Christ called them and not man. We need to forsake what we love and value most when Christ calls us if we are to experience God's move, which fights fear. What do you value so much that you cannot forsake it for Christ's sake like these people did? Just imagine if they reasoned with Him that "there is this and that for me to accomplish first before coming to You, Lord." Obviously they would have missed the promotion of being fishers of men.

Are you missing God's promotion because of your arguments related to fear? Is He calling you to full-time ministry? Maybe you reason out that you first need to get married, educate children, and achieve earthly materials before hearkening to His call because you fear you will lose and will feel better off the way you are. You know better. Be careful lest you lose your spiritual and eternal promotion just because of those temporary worldly possessions you desire first. Take a step immediately when He calls you, just as these people did; after all, the word states clearly, "But seek ye first the kingdom of God and his righteousness; and all these things shall be added unto you. Take therefore no thought for the morrow: for the morrow shall take thought for the things of itself. Sufficient unto the day is the evil thereof" (Matthew 6:33–34). Cast out all fear and regard the Lord, and you will never regret it.

Another thing to note in these people is that they *left their father* without fear of what others would say about them. Just imagine leaving a father whom God used to bring you into this world of the sun. Surely this sums up all we need to forsake and leave for Christ's sake without fretting. They left him with the hired servants, who couldn't inherit him. Our obedience to God's call is no joke because we must leave all we value, such as our jobs, parents, children, husbands, and so forth if we are to get spiritual promotions. Also note keenly from the above scriptures the words *immediately* and *straightway*. These words give us no time to reason or seek advice from our beloved ones or next of kin.

It's a matter of individuality because God will never force anybody into His service. Further, we note that after they obeyed to follow Christ, they witnessed the mighty works Christ did at Capernaum. Fearing to take immediate action when Christ calls us prevents our seeing or experiencing God's move, even in other people's lives. Fear not, my friend, as you hastily obey the Lord. It's worth it all with no regrets, but there are benefits here on earth and also in heaven.

> And they went into Capernaum and straightway on the Sabbath day he entered into the synagogue, and taught. And they were astonished at his doctrine: for he taught them as one that had authority, and not as scribes. And there was in their synagogue a man with an unclean spirit; and he cried out saying, Let

## Fear Not; God Is in Charge

us alone: what have we to do with thee, thou Jesus of Nazareth? Art thou come to destroy us? I know thee who thou art, the Holy one of God. And Jesus rebuked him, saying, Hold thy peace, and come out of him. And when the unclean Spirit had torn him, and cried with a loud voice, he came out of him. And they were all amazed, insomuch that they questioned among themselves, saying, what thing is this? What new doctrine is this? for with authority commanded he even the unclean spirits, and they do obey him. And immediately his fame spread abroad throughout the entire region round about Galilee." (Mark 1:21–28)

After they obeyed without fear, they were more encouraged when in His company, with all Jesus did wherever they went, and their faith increased. When we obey the Lord fearlessly, we will mature from one step of glory to another as we experience God's move in our lives as we serve Him. Fighting fear is experiencing spiritual growth. Do you feel like you are spiritually retarded? Check on whether you entertain worries, especially in obedience. Fear of the future takes a burden beyond your human capability. Leave it to God, who knows your future. He knows about tomorrow and what you will be undergoing. Stop doing what you aren't able to control. Trust God, who knows all, and stop fearing, and all those things that have been arduous to you will be well in the Lord's care.

Later Jesus openly told His disciples about the need for self-denial if any wished to follow Him. "And when he had called the people unto him with his disciples also, he said unto them, whosoever will come after me, let him *deny himself* and take up his cross and follow me. For whosoever will *save his life* shall *lose it*; but whosoever shall *lose his life* for my sake and the gospel's, the same *shall save it*" (Mark 8:34–35, emphasis added). Denying ourselves casts out fear because we will be so focused on the Lord that we will have no time to fear.

Have you denied yourself for the Lord? If not, you must fear in one way or the other. Surrender all to Him, and it will be taken care of.

Meditating on God's word fights fear very easily, and it's all we need when we deny ourselves. Today we can witness or experience God's mighty works in us and through us only when we obey and forsake our valuable status and possessions for God's kingdom sake. Our God isn't so unrighteous as to forget our good works; hence there is no way He can make us lose when we are serving Him fully. If you limit God in service, He will also limit His blessings and presence to you. Our God is a democratic God who gives us what we deserve after choosing what to do since He has given every human being the capacity to choose to obey or disobey Him, and each is always rewarded accordingly. He will never force anybody to obey, but He likes us to do so willingly. He will never treat us like robots, which are always controlled. "Be ye not deceived; God is not mocked: for whatsoever a man soweth, that shall he also reap" (Galatians 6:7). If you serve God more, you will be more blessed; and if you serve Him meanly, the same will be the blessings and even the anointing.

Our Lord Jesus is so considerate to us because He comprehends when we leave all for His sake, and no wonder He made it plain and clear to His own disciples when He told them, "Verily I say unto you, There is no man that hath left house, or parents, or brethren or wife or children, for the Kingdom of God's sake, who shall not receive manifold more in this present time and in the world to come life Everlasting" (Luke 18:29–30). Then fearing is like fooling ourselves since we always gain when we obey God. I thank God so much that He is such a faithful God. It is here on earth, not only in heaven, that we have to receive manifold more. So fear not as you serve God because God is working all on your behalf. Many Christians who don't study the word well are deceived that they must live miserable lives on earth with all sorts of fear as they await the heavenly pay. My friend, I challenge you now to read the word of God to stand firm and know your rights both here and for the life to come, and all are against fear.

I believe with all my heart that we Christians should live the best lives on earth if we properly read the word and live the same word. We are supposed to be high above in all we do as we obey God and His word. God keeps our respective accounts of everything we

## Fear Not; God Is in Charge

leave behind when we are out to serve Him. So He obviously expects us to leave them. Fathers and mothers are being called to leave their families for God's sake on missionary work, not just leaving for their own businesses, which many are capable of. Many fear what people in their neighborhood speculate if they hear of their departure for missions while leaving their families behind. This is a bell the enemy loudly rings to call you into idleness for God's work, and I warn you to watch out because the harvest is ready, but there is a big shortage of laborers. I know many women who received scholarship abroad, and they left their little ones, even as young as five months. Why don't they fear what people say when they leave for that pursuit?

Just think of other people you know who have in one time left their dear ones for wordily things, yet when one obeys the voice of God, the devil comes preaching nonsense. Fear not as you obey the Lord. I work in an office, and every time I return to work after maternity leave, I always leave my small one at a very tender age of two months and resume the job, which provides for only worldly pay. Oh, how hypocritical we behave before God as we reason that we shouldn't leave our beloved for the sake of the kingdom. Fear not as you go to further the gospel of the kingdom. Fight fear in Jesus's name and be fruitful as Christ requires you. He is calling all into the battlefield—not just one sex but all who will hearken to take the gospel of good tidings.

Women, of whom I am, fear not as you serve the Lord. Your reward awaits you in heaven. God asked, "Whom shall I send and who will go for us?" (Isaiah 6:8). He never specified men but any human being with flesh and blood who is ready to hearken to the voice of the Lord, not only men. Today people are slowly reversing the scriptures because most missionary work seems to be left to the youth or to the ones who have already finished their delicate parental work. Men also go out, and we stick to our traditions so much that women are always left at home, but I thank God that women have a very crucial role in the service of God. Women were the first people to witness the resurrection of Jesus as they went to the tomb very early in the morning. Mary Magdalene, Joanna, Mary, the mother of James, and other women were with them.

> Now upon the first day of the week, very early in the morning, they came unto the sepulcher, bringing spices which they had prepared, and certain others with them. And they found the stone Rolled away from the sepulcher. And they entered in and found not the body of the Lord Jesus. And it came to pass, as they were much perplexed thereabout, behold, two men stood by them in shining Garments: And as they were afraid, and bowed down their faces to the earth, they said unto them, why seek ye the living among the dead? He is not here, but is risen: remember how he spoke unto you when he was yet in Galilee, saying, The son of man must be delivered into the hands of sinful men, and be crucified, and the third day rise again. And they remembered his words and returned from the sepulchre, and told all these things unto the eleven, and to all the rest. It was Mary Magdalene, and Joanna, and Mary the mother of James and other women that were with them, which told these things unto the apostles. And their words seemed to them as *idle tales* and they believed them not. (Luke 24:1–11, emphasis added)

Men always struggle to believe women's reports on the first instance, even as we note these disciples. Many things men regard as nonsense from women are very crucial and of spiritual benefit, even today. From this text, we note the following vital phrases, which carry heavy words in meaning:

1. Very early in the morning
2. They came
3. Bringing spices

4. They entered in
5. Bowed down their faces to the ground
6. Remembered his words
7. Told all these things unto the eleven and to all the rest

Let's look at these in detail.

## Very Early in the Morning

Clearly they forsook their beds and the very sweet sleep of the early-morning hours. Very early to me is like before dawn, and it's normally very chilly outside, yet these women purposed to go that early to the tomb because Christ was more valuable than sleep to them. They didn't mind that they were just mere women because they knew status and sexuality were immaterial to God. There is more than our sexual status before God. Our commitment is what counts, whether one is a man or a woman. A woman can be of more benefit before the eyes of God if she is obedient to God's call and word than just a man who is bound by traditions of the time as being head or a leader. A man would seem puerile before God if he relied on only being the head or leader and not on doing anything for God.

Our God is a doing God, and He appreciates doing people, men and women alike. May God help us to get out of our cultural cocoons, which only hinder the word of God and the power thereof. These women did what was good in the sight of God. Regardless of whether the culture of their time approved of them, they purposed to obey God rather than man, leaving their sweet sleep in favor of Christ, their Savior. We also need to forsake what we value in our daily lives in favor of our God. The time you need most is what God would appreciate more than just serving Him only when you have nothing else to do or only when it's convenient for you. God doesn't need your spare time because He also doesn't give you spare blessings or favor. Others value their jobs more than service to God because they dare to sleep in on Sundays when they should be busy serving God, in contrast to weekdays when they prepare in haste not to be late for their jobs.

I challenge you to put your priorities right. Be careful lest you behave like the Romans, whom Paul warned because of their behavior of exchanging priorities. "Because that, when they knew God, they glorified him not as God, neither were thankful; but became vain in their imaginations, and their foolish heart was darkened. Professing themselves to be wise, they became fools and changed the glory of the incorruptible God into an image made like to corruptible man, and to birds, and four footed beasts, and creeping things, who changed the truth of God into a lie and worshipped and served the creature more than the creator, who is the blessed forever Amen" (Romans 1:21–23, 25). Many times we regard the very big sins, but it's more sinful to give preference to earthly things and commitments than to our God. It's the same thing the Romans were doing regarding what God had created instead of the Creator Himself. Imagine your job and your God. He is the giver of life; you leave alone other things like jobs, yet the enemy continues to lure you every Sunday morning to sleep a bit. Why not sleep a bit during working days? May God help us to wake up spiritually.

Even today many people love sleep so much that they had better miss morning devotions or be late to attend first church services than miss their sweet sleep on a Sunday morning. I challenge you, if you are such a Christian, be like these women, and you will be blessed more in the church than in your bed. As mothers, they must have left behind their husbands and children for the sake of Christ, the Savior. We also need to follow their footsteps of leaving those very close things we cling to in life for the sake of Christ and the gospel. Women today always use their children as scapegoats when it comes to service for God. Children are only gifts from God, the Creator, yet you say you cannot serve him because of your children. So you might have been better off without them, yet God is able to take them away, so you serve Him if they are a hindrance. Alternatively, you can bring them up to be only thieves, fornicators, and so forth.

Set your spiritual priorities right now, and I promise you will never once regret them, because our God is faithful, even when we fail to be so. He still remains faithful because that's His nature. Get the revelation and give Him the right place in your life and all you have; after all, you aren't your own. He bought you with a price, His only begotten Son, Jesus Christ. Imagine early in the morning before children wake up. This sounds awkward, but to the women, it was all right. The very awkward things realistically are the rightful things spiritually, like Abraham going to sacrifice his only son, Isaac, whom he had gotten from God in his old age. Doesn't killing your own son sound funny and realistically awkward? Yet God wanted it that way for His glory. Women, let's rise early in the morning and seek the Lord in prayer, pray for the lost to have a desire for the redeemer, pray for the ministers of the gospel, pray for the street children, pray for nations and their leaders since we are expected to lead peaceful and quiet lives. Marriages are in a great mess since the enemy is out to shatter them through various venues of mistrust and infidelity, financial strains, interference by in-laws, communication breakdowns, and so forth. The Lord still encourages women in His service with a "Fear not" because He is with us.

## They Came

This phrase shows me that they left their ordinary places of residence and went to the tomb. We also need to leave our ordinary residences to go out in search of our Savior. These places could be churches where we can hear the word of God, fellowship with others who have come for the same reason, and overnight prayer meetings (*keshas*), where we can pray and cry before our maker in worship and so forth. Christ also lived a life of prayer and used to isolate Himself to pray; prayer was the secret of His effective ministry. Leaving their residences shows they were committed to their Savior. To date, women are so committed, and no wonder they get married and are committed to their husbands. Their commitment is well illustrated because they never left Christ, even to the cross (Luke 8). They encouraged Him as He carried the cross all the way to the grave. Imagine that they didn't even know He was going to rise again, yet they still committed themselves to His dead body.

Today Christ is already risen and seated at the right hand of the Father in heaven. So you dare not miss committing yourself to Him. If we enjoy prayers answered now, how much more shall we enjoy serving Him in full commitment? Be committed to Him and His work now. Be well informed and have the legs to go to that place where there are those sinners waiting for your word as you engage in evangelism. Remember the question to Isaiah—"Whom shall I send?" He is asking the same question now, and it's a privilege to be used of God and a blessing too—both to your life and to those whom you will be sent. It's never too late to start. Now is the time for you to be commissioned but at will because God requires willing vessels who aren't going to serve Him for the sake of merely doing.

## Bringing Spices

As clearly written, the women brought their spices. We also need to give our properties for the sake of our commitment to Christ. There can never be any commitment without the giving of something. The word indicates that they had prepared these spices, so they worked on the body's preparation by giving of their time and efforts, yet they brought them to the tomb for the master's body. What we have worked on, spent our materials on, is still needed today as we come to the Lord. Maybe you ask, "How?" I will answer this way, and I believe you will consent with me: Once you get saved, you give your entire life to Christ, and no wonder Paul said that for the sake of knowing Christ, "I have counted all others as a loss."

We should also do the same if we entirely give our lives to Christ. *Entirely* means even what you have. So if we have entirely given ourselves to God, we won't be reluctant to give, whether we have possessions, time, strength for the service of the Lord, and so forth. Many times Christians tend to behave like small children. If you buy them candy and give them, then you happen to request may be for just a piece of the candy; they will be reluctant as they hold them tightly in their hands. They forget that were it not for your generosity to them, they wouldn't have those sweets. Here I take material possessions God has blessed us with as the sweets and human beings as the small children.

Many Christians, after being blessed, hold so tightly to their given blessings to some extent that even tithing is a big problem, let alone other church offerings and commitments, because they fear to lose some of their riches. Fear not as you give to God, because He is the giver of all you have. Even today spices are very precious, but those women couldn't compare their value to their Savior's dead body. How much more then do we need to give willingly to our living master, Jesus? We can speculate that these women were taking their spices to the dead body of their Savior and had even forgotten that He had told them He would resurrect. So they were just valuing His dead body like any other person who dies, but they honored their walk with Him while he was alive. May God help us to know we have nothing of our own, but all is from God and to us through His Son, Jesus Christ, which should motivate us to surrender all to him.

When they entered in, they found the stone rolled away from the sepulcher, and *they entered in* and found not the body of the Lord (vv. 2–3, emphasis added). These three words "they entered in" mean so much to me, and I believe if you also endeavor to analyze them properly, they can be of much teaching to you today. Suppose they just saw the stone rolled away and feared to enter in; what could have happened? *Courage* here is the key word, and so we need to be courageous in this journey, even as we meet different situations in this life, even as is the title of this book. Fear is a great menace in Christianity today, and we need to spiritually and courageously fight it if we expect any success. No wonder the word says, "But the fearful, and unbelieving, and the abominable, and murderers and where mongers, and sorcerers, and idolaters, and all Liars shall have their part in the lake which burneth with fire and brimstone which is the second death" (Revelation 21:8). I sometimes note that fear is more dangerous than witchcraft because it's fear that prompts one to do such things, and the Holy Spirit gave me a deep revelation that if we overcome fear, we are able to overcome all other obstacles. From the above quotation, we see that fear is the first "the fearful." It's the fearful who will proceed while unbelieving; it's the fearful who will abominate because they cannot just hate without a cause. Fear of being defeated brings hatred; the fearful murder because they endeavor to eliminate some characters they speculate are obstacles to their success. The fearful become warmongers, as they find their way to succeed in malicious ways. Fearfulness makes people think that if they destabilize other people's lives through sorcery, they will achieve what they desire. Fear leads people to idol worshipping, thinking they will be provided with what they need through idolatry; fear leads to lying as people think they can easily escape by hiding the truth. Our knowing who Jesus is and what He means in our lives should make us fight fear because He turns the negative to positive, our being in bondage to freedom, our sadness to gladness, our defeat to victory, and even our darkness to light. That is because Christ is God's additional factor to add whatever the enemy subtracts, as God planned from the beginning. Fear not because with Jesus, you become a child of God and also more than a conqueror. Therefore, we see these are the results of fear. Fight fear in Jesus's name, because the fearful won't inherit the kingdom of God. These women entered in fearlessly because they knew their stand in the Lord.

We can enter into ministry of the gospel only if we eliminate fear. We can enter the church, trusting God to minister to our very personal needs if we eliminate fear. We can enter a room where there are sick people in a delirium to be prayed for if we don't have fear; we can reach high-ranked people with the gospel as we profess Christ if we don't dread. We can share our hassles with our pastors or counselors for counseling if we don't dread what they will think of us. And the list of examples is endless.

## Bowed Down Their Faces to the Earth

After they missed the body of their Savior, they were much perplexed and bowed their faces to the earth. It was a sign of sorrow that made them to do so. When we are sorrowful about our surroundings and displeasing situations, we can bow our faces as we seek the Lord in prayer and humility. I believe they bowed their faces and cried in prayer for their missing Lord's body. In this life, when we miss the mark, we need to sorrowfully seek God in prayer, who will always provide an angel to comfort us with an encouraging answer. For these women, two men stood by them in shining garments (angels) and later said to them, "Why seek ye the living among the dead?" When we bow our faces, sorrowing in prayer, angels will always come with comforting words, assuring us of the victory through whom we seek, Jesus. Instead of complaining, they sought the face of God. We should also seek God's face when we encounter hassles instead of complaining like those without hope in God do. Instead of fearing, we should pray to God and be encouraged that we shall be rewarded because God is a rewarder of those who diligently seek Him.

## Remembered His Words

They were carefully listening to their master when He was with them, and the words they heard from Him quickened in their minds, and they immediately remembered the angels mentioned. The word of God is true. This truth should teach us the importance of having the word of God in us, which the Holy Spirit can quicken at the hour of need. To have the word in us is to read the Bible, and the devil will never have a chance of misleading us, as he does to those who never take time for the word and blindly follow his dark ways, which lead them to eternal damnation. The word of God should dwell richly in us; we should meditate on the word of God always, and the same will be like chewing the cud when the need arises. To go to God, you don't need to be learned or have a degree. God's degree is heeding His words. "My son, attend to my words; incline thine ear unto my sayings let Them not depart from thine eyes; keep them in the midst of thine heart. For they are life unto those that find them, and health to all their flesh" (Proverbs 4:20–22).

These women heeded the sayings of Jesus when He was with them, and the same assisted them when they were in great need of comfort. In the same way, it is the word we hear, study, meditate on, and heed that will comfort us when we are discouraged. The work of the Holy Spirit is manifested in such times because He reminds us of a scripture we read or heard from the Bible, and we are able to face the challenge fearlessly. When the challenges of life come, the word will give us victory, as was the case of David and Goliath. The word gave David victory irrespective of his small status compared to that of Goliath, who was very mighty. No matter how big the problem is, the right word will bring victory when applied correctly, and mind you there is always a word for every circumstance you encounter.

"Then David said to the Philistine, Thou comest to me with a sword, and with a spear, and with a shield but I come to thee in the name of the Lord of hosts the God of the armies of Israel whom thou hast defied" (1 Samuel 17:45). David was confident of His God, and every attempt to stop him was a dead one. We need to be confident of our God through His holy word, and victory will be ours. He is the same yesterday, today, and forever. He is the Lord who changes not. Men may change, but He will never, neither His promises because they are yea and amen. He isn't a man that He should lie, neither a son of man that He should repent of every promise He has given us as His children, whom He purchased with the precious blood of His only Son, Jesus Christ. In all these, spiritually drowsy people will hardly attain any victory since the enemy will make them complacent of all situations they go through. May God help you and me to avoid being spiritually flimsy in this journey.

## They told all these things unto the eleven and all the rest

These women embarked on evangelistic work. Amen. I get excited more here because women were the first evangelists. The devil has cheated our generation for so long, but those who read the word well have caught him. Women should evangelize more than any other people. I get thrilled when I see women of our time holding microphones in big crusades and giving the word of Christ the way these women did. Women, where are you? Come on and get involved if you haven't yet started and tell those who aren't yet saved that Christ is risen from the grave, that Christ is healing the sick of their diverse sicknesses, delivering the captives, and so forth. You should be the first to evangelize your family, church, nation, and worldwide because God's vision is a world vision. "Making the word of God of none effect through your tradition which ye have delivered: and many such like things do ye" (Mark 7:13).

What is happening to the ministry of women? Our tradition has been teaching us that women should be at home, but glory be to God that the word is plain and clear. Our traditions are making the word of none effect if we believe women should always be at home. Women should wake up early, go to the tomb where the work is, take their valuables, enter where there is work, bow down their faces as they plead for the lost souls in prayers, remember God's word about the work, and go everywhere, telling others, "Repent for the kingdom of God is at hand." Jesus went to visit Martha and Mary, and immediately when he entered the house, Martha did like any other woman. She continued to be in the kitchen and even complained to Jesus that Mary wasn't bothered to assist her in the kitchen work. I like the way Jesus answered her. "Martha, Martha, thou art careful and troubled about many things, but one thing is needful and Mary hath chosen that good part, which shall not be taken away from her."

Mary had chosen a different path of staying at the feet of Jesus, and Martha found it odd for a woman to behave that way in the house; furthermore, when there was a visitor to be catered for, kitchen matters were first. Even today, women have always been victims in this field. Once visitors arrive, the good woman of that particular house greets them, warmly welcomes them, and makes a comment like, "Just feel at home and excuse me a bit." With that she is quickly back in the kitchen, struggling to prepare what is available, and tea is the most commonly prepared thing. All this is good, but I tend to think Mary's style is best, first sitting with the visitors and encouraging one another since they or you might need the spiritual nourishment more than the tea. The time factor at the same time may be against all of you. Maybe whatever brought them to you was just counseling, which should be attended to first before the physical side with the tea or food. So if you happen to visit me and I start sharing what God is doing in my life and teaching me from His word, please don't mistake me for being mean. I prefer Mary's style to that of Martha, and I find it to be valuable, especially if my visitors are in a hurry. What we bother ourselves with is temporal, but the word of encouragement will be forever. Fear not as you provide the spiritual nourishment first.

> The Lord our God spoke unto us in Horeb, saying, Ye have dwelt long enough in this mount; Turn you and take your journey, and go to the mount of the Amorites, and unto all the places nigh thereunto, in the plain, in the hills, and in the vale, and in the south and by the sea side, to the land of the Canaanites, and unto Lebanon, unto the great river, the river Euphrates. (Deuteronomy 1:7–7)

> Ye have compassed this mountain long enough; turn you northward and command thou the people, saying, Ye are to pass through the coast of your brethren the children of Esau, which dwell in Seir; and they shall be afraid of you: take ye good heed unto yourselves therefore: meddle not with them; for I will not give you of their land, no not so much as a foot breadth: because I have given mount Seir unto Esau of a possession. (Deuteronomy 2:3–5)

Here, we see the Israelites were being told what they had been doing for a long time. We are the Israelites of the day, and we have stayed long enough in houses. It isn't wrong, but we also need to be out on missions like the women who went to the tomb to anoint the dead body of Jesus. Our homes are like the mountain where the Israelites stayed for long, and the Lord is urging us to turn and take our journey as these women did. The mountains of the Amorites can be symbolic of the sinners in the world who live under the control of the prince of darkness, the devil. The unevangelized regions are given to us, even as Christ commissioned His disciples to go into *all* the nations and not to *some* parts of the nations, preaching the gospel of the kingdom. Suppose they continued staying where they were, just enjoying the fellowship of their master. If so, who could have gone to preach? If you stay in your warm fellowship of believers and attend every church meeting for encouragement without going out to give what has been given in your Jerusalem (church), who will reach the lost outside? If we don't do the great commission Christ has given us, then we will be doing the great omission of not taking the gospel to the unreached. This as a result delays the coming of Christ because it is after all hear the gospel that Christ will return.

Sometimes I have wondered about constipation. It comes after taking too much food, which, if not discarded, becomes a sickness problem. There are different ways to discard of food biologically; once you eat, after the proper digestion, some food is absorbed into the blood for the benefit of the body. The unwanted waste is discarded as feces. If too much food is taken wrongly, it is normally discarded by vomiting, and one is relieved of that major problem. Spiritually, I have wondered many times, and I ask myself several unanswered questions up to now on how spiritual people don't suffer spiritual constipation after being well nourished in the church with fellowships and all other good Christian meetings.

Naturally, if you eat properly, the food will be digested normally and absorbed into the bloodstream for the help of a healthy body without any complications. Spiritually, when we feed well, we should be healthy and be able to give the word out nicely in a balanced manner.

Unfortunately, many tend to relax too much and are still being fed every now and then as they attend fellowships, church meetings, and church services. Then there arises a spiritual constipation. As mentioned earlier, constipation biologically is very uncomfortable, and one feels fatigued by the same. Spiritual constipation can be noted in many churches today and in many Christians because if you fail to give out the word to the right people, the same will be hazardous to the entire body of Christ. As a result, you get rumor mongering in the church and all other discouraging behaviors because Christians are so full, and the only thing one can do is vomit anyhow. I hope you will believe me that if you are from a church service and have no business of going out for God in the company of a colleague of your caliber, there is a tendency for you to analyze the sermon you both heard in the church. You start diverting it to another church member as you say, "I wish so-and-so was there because that sermon was his." The word, being inspired by God, always comes to reprove, correct, and even instruct. "All scripture is given by inspiration of God and is profitable for doctrine, for reproof, for correction, for instruction in righteousness" (2 Timothy 3:16). God is not like man; He is always faithful. And so He can't just bring a word through His servant for an absent person. How will such a person hear? Individuality is vital in all spiritual realms if any proper nourishment is to be effected.

A healthy spiritual life exists when a Christian hears a message and starts practicing the same without much idleness because idleness is a character Satan looks to fill with all his dirty plans, thoughts, and actions. If the message is on commission, embark on commission work for God. If it's on giving, start giving. If it's on patience, start practicing patience in your life and so forth. Women, fear not the whispers of the enemy that women should be silent in church. Paul was writing to a church that had the problem of women not respecting their husbands; therefore, they were forbidden to talk in public. Our churches, where women are taught about their rightful biblical responsibilities, have no problem, and so we can continue with the great commission. Nevertheless, there is a vital thing to know as women; whether we are evangelists or pastors in the missionary work, in our homes we remain wives under the leadership of our husbands, on whom God has bestowed responsibility. These husbands should also lead us in the ways of God and not traditionally, a fact many men, even Christians, have mistaken. When we read the word and live by its standards, all will be done harmoniously without misunderstandings, which the enemy brings if he notes ignorance of the word in our lives. May God help us to live by the word in all we set to do for the glory of God, and we shall not fear.

I mention this because the Bible warns us against giving the devil a chance (Ephesians 4:27). A uninformed woman evangelist may foolishly start binding demons in the house if her husband annoys her. This isn't right. In the house, we are under the headship of our husbands, and any bragging behavior should be avoided to glorify God in all ways and everywhere by taking our rightful positions. Another problem and confusion come when husbands lead not in the ways of the Lord but in the traditional ways. As mentioned earlier in this book, the traditions of men make the word of God to be of no effect. May God help our good husbands to lead and guide us in our homes in the way of the Lord. Many deny their wives permission to serve God without any good reason just because they are the head of the house. I believe the word has enough provision for every situation and everybody, so it will be of great help if a husband who fears God sits down and reasons out with the wives nicely and in a respectful manner if a mission has been canceled. Then all will be solved amicably and peacefully.

Once, I was supposed to go on a mission with a particular evangelistic group. It was in our home area. Two days prior to departure, my husband told me I couldn't go, but he made me comprehend, as he reasoned, that it wasn't wise for me to go empty handed to my parents' home. I consented with a good heart because he made me understand the situation, which financial obstacles affected. Little did I know that God had a very good reason and plan beyond the finances, which I believe He had allowed deliberately to teach me His ways later.

The team went and ministered, but somehow things went wrong somewhere because they went beyond the doctrines of the church hosting the mission. The outcome was that they couldn't go there again to preach. Later, I was invited to the same place to minister, and God has continued to open more doors to date, even for my other colleagues, to share the word of God in the same church to different departments of that church. Suppose I had ignored my husband's reason for not allowing me to go that first time. I couldn't have managed to have a way through later. Here, I know the spirit of an uninformed evangelist would have motivated him or her to quote the words in the Bible on violence as recorded in Mathew 11:12, but if you are mature spiritually, you will agree with me that obedience is better than sacrifice in the eyes of God. All things work together for good.

We weren't stable financially, and God had allowed it so that I could get more chances of serving Him in that church. Be stable in the word, and all things will always leave you more informed on the things of God in the spiritual realm and for the glory of His holy name. If God calls us to reason with Him as sinners, how much more do we need to reason among ourselves? "Come now, let us reason together, saith the Lord: though your sins be as scarlet, they shall be as white as snow; though they be red like crimson, they shall be as wool" (Isaiah 1:18).

I heard many complaints when in women's meetings during counseling and question times, from women who were refused permission for no good reason. Their husbands just said, "You aren't going to that meeting or mission, and I have said it as the head of this house!" Surely such a brutal statement and order will leave the weaker vessel, as the Bible regards women, broken down and discouraged with only the all-gracious God to console.

> Speaking to yourselves in psalms and hymns and spiritual songs, singing and making melody in your heart to the Lord; Giving thanks Always for all things unto God and the Father in the name of our Lord Jesus Christ; Submitting yourselves one to another in the fear of God. Wives, submit yourselves unto your own husbands, as unto the Lord. For the husband is

## Fear Not; God Is in Charge

the head of the wife, even as Christ is the head of the church: and he is the savior of the body. Therefore as the church is subject unto Christ, so let the wives be to their own husbands in everything. Husbands, love your wives, even as Christ also loved the church, and gave himself for it. (Ephesians 5:19–25)

These words, if followed the way they are, can bring peace and harmony in the family. *"Submitting yourselves one to another in the fear of God"* (v. 21, emphasis added). Grammatically they indicate pluralism. Both parties are to submit each one to the other. This submission calls for the sacrifice of each party, which is a missing ingredient in most Christian marriages and hence the chaos we get or experience for that matter. If you are married or if you normally share with married people, you will comprehend this better. I thank God that He comprehends our sinful and weak nature in us as human beings because of the words "in the fear of God."

Realistically, submitting ourselves to each other in a normal way isn't easy; hence the Bible admonishes us to do so in the fear of God. It is when a husband fears God and the wife respectively that submitting will be easy and smooth. Should there be one *not in the fear of God*, submission will always exist in friction, needing some grease to smooth it. This grease I see as the Spirit and the grace of God. By this I mean that it would take the grace of God for a normal woman to submit with a good heart to a brutal husband, who gives orders traditionally and not biblically. The Bible tells us that when one is in Christ, he or she is a new creature. A new creature, I believe, should actually be the really new creature, who may have been dominated by tradition and manhood and now is new, in that grace abounds much, even in homes especially for the man as the head of the house.

Similarly, it would also take the grace of God for a normal man, especially in other cultures like Africa, to submit to the wife, even when he is a born-again Christian. The tradition expects him to be head more in ordering than in taking action. Everybody—man or woman, saved or not—will agree with me that our men today are very good at giving orders but very poor in doing their god-given responsibilities, and this is the main reason for the many marriage problems we see among pastors, evangelist, counselors, wives, children, the community as a whole, and so forth. Initially, God wanted a woman to be a helper to the man, but the whole thing has been interchanged; and hence we see the many problems being experienced. Many readers may feel challenged by this, but this is nothing but the truth, which many times hurts.

Women, I challenge you as your fellow woman to wake up and leave your children for the sake of the gospel; life will never be the same anymore. I have personally experienced the joy of serving and leaving my little children behind for the sake of taking the good news. The Bible excites my heart when I read, "How beautiful are the feet of them that preach the gospel of peace and bring good tidings of good things" (Romans 10:15). Do you want your feet to be counted as beautiful? Embark, leaving your family, and take the gospel of the Lord Jesus Christ out to the unreached and the regions beyond. Leaving isn't neglecting, hating, or divorcing if you are leaving for the sake of the gospel. Children are so close to parents, yet we are expected to leave them when the Savior needs us. I believe with all my heart that when the little ones who need the presence of both parents more, especially the mother, are left for missionary work, our almighty God's healing, nursing, and so forth in our absence for the glory of His name will make them well catered for. When we are on business for God, He will surely be busy commanding the angels to attend to our needs in our absence.

As mentioned earlier, I serve God in singing, and I also evangelize the lost souls in the world. So most of the times during weekends, more often than not, I am out on missions when I am expected to be with my family. All the same, I still leave them. I was a mother of two children who were then six and four years old respectively, and I started leaving them when they were three and one years old. For some missions, I used to go with the younger one when she was very small, even when she was breastfeeding, and I always saw God take care of her, especially in the late hours while in revival meetings. Many mothers are aware that if small kids are exposed to cold weather, they can easily catch a cold, but God always protected mine. Glory be to his holy name. You will attend all meetings, and your kid will be healthier than those whose mothers cared for them at home. The reason is that you are out doing God's business, not yours. Amen.

At first, my children cried when I left them, especially early in the morning if I had to travel a long distance of maybe two or three hours before the appointed mission time. Leaving was painful for me too, but I had to do so for the sake of the commission, and I believe this is why Paul said that the way of the cross is foolishness to those who perish, but it is power to those who believe. So whatever your status, don't undermine your capability because God is always looking for laborers, and many highly esteemed people of status are normally very busy in their businesses, which prevent their availability for God's work.

# Chapter 4

# Fear Not as You Give

THROUGHOUT MY SERVICE for God, I have learned that giving is costly. We shouldn't fret as we give because God Himself, who is our creator, is the author of giving. He gave us the best, His only-begotten Son, Jesus Christ. We also need to give the best to God, even as we serve Him.

First, we must give ourselves fully to Him by accepting His precious gift, Christ, to save us. That is the initial step of giving to God. No matter how much you serve God, without surrendering your entire life to Him, be well informed that you haven't yet squared things with Him as He expects. It was costly for God to give us His only Son. Therefore, we must realize that our giving cannot be giving until it costs us something. As we serve in whichever way, we must count the cost if it's going to be effective at all. Let's look further at the following reference:

> And David, according to the saying of God, went up as the Lord commanded. And Araunah looked, and saw the king and his servants coming toward him: and Araunah went out, and bowed himself before the king on his face upon the ground. And Araunah said, wherefore is my lord the king come to his servants?

## Fear Not; God Is in Charge

And David said, to buy the threshing floor of thee, to build an altar unto the Lord, that the plague may be stayed from the people. And Araunah said unto David, let my lord the king take and offer up what seemeth good unto him: behold, here be oxen for burnt sacrifice, and threshing instruments and other instruments of the oxen for wood. All these things did Araunah as a king, give unto the king, And Araunah said unto the King, the Lord thy God accept thee. And the king said unto Araunah, Nay *but I will surely buy it of thee at a price: neither will I offer burnt offerings unto the lord my god of that which doth cost me nothing.* "So David bought the threshing floor and the oxen for fifty shekels of silver. And David built there an altar unto the Lord, and offered burnt offerings and peace offerings. So the Lord was entreated for the land, and the plague was stayed from Israel" (2 Samuel 24:19–25)

From this text, we see that David purposed in his heart to offer to God what costed him something. King Araunah offered it to him free, but David preferred to buy it at a price, because he knew whom he believed and served—that God desired more of his own things not those offered by others.

I wonder, if the threshing floor and everything King Araunah offered David were offered to you today, would you choose the way David did? Let's be ready to offer what costs us something to our dear loving father in heaven, who gave the best for our redemption, Jesus Christ, His only Son. Many are in the habit of giving God leftovers like He is a dog. Stop doing that and give Him what costs you something (for example, strength, time, money, service, and so forth). Also a rich man may give to the work of God, but he still has much left over. To him that gift isn't really giving that costs him much. On the other hand, a poor person may give only a small amount to the same work of God, and maybe, before he gave it out, which might have been reserved for his return ticket to his home or for another vital use. In spite of having other pressing financial needs, he chose to give for God's work. To me that is giving that cost him something. He may even walk back home if the money was meant for fare.

Jesus Christ taught this truth about sacrifice when He told the parable of the widow who gave all she had. "And He looked up and saw the rich men casting their gifts into the treasury. And He saw also a certain poor widow casting in thither two mites and He said, of a truth I say unto you, that this poor widow hath cast in more than they all. For all these have of their abundance cast in unto the offerings of God; but she of her penury hath cast in *all the living that she had*" (Luke 21:1–4, emphasis added)

Your giving must cost you something for it to count as true giving before God. It's not how much you give that counts but how much you give of yourself before God and how much it costs you. The previous text about King David and Araunah puts us on the same page. What does it cost you even as you serve God? It must cost you something when you give to God in whichever way. For sure, if it costs you much, then it's worth something before God. As you provide for the needy around you, it must cost you some of the things you would keep for your own need, and the same will be giving that costs you something.

Many people like giving only when they are in plenty, but giving that costs you something occurs even when you are in need, yet you give. As you tithe, do you first start with your daily needs, or do you separate your tithe first? If so, then know it isn't giving that costs you much. The phrase "God will understand" has caught many unaware and made them treat God like a beggar. Just because your needs are more than the supply, you make yourself to believe that God will understand if you don't tithe that particular month.

In such a case, start with the tithe and let God take care of your other pressing needs because "God first and all other things follow" is the proper principle that will make you not lack at any particular time. That will be tithing that costs you something, and you will be blessed, even as it is "more blessed to give than to receive." God will be no man's debtor, so if you make your tithe your first priority, it will be

## Fear Not; God Is in Charge

like challenging God on His promises, and He will surely act on your faithfulness. Remember Abraham when he acted on the voice of God to sacrifice his only son, Isaac. It was after God saw that Abraham honored Him that He provided the lamb for the sacrifice instead of the beheading of Isaac. At the eleventh hour, it was provided. The knife was already lifted, but before landing on Isaac's neck, God intervened. That was giving that cost Abraham something.

Do your daily needs so press you? Honor God, the giver of all including your own life with tithes first, and at the time when you speculate you will be financially stuck, the intervention of God will surprise you. Tithing that costs you something will make the plague of poverty be removed. The devourer will be rebuked on your behalf. Fear not as you give to God. because He requires only a small fraction of all He has given us.

Giving is living because the more you give, the more you get without your supplying source running out. A flowing river has fresh water because it always gives out as it flows. If you need flesh blessings daily, start to give, and you will witness that God never promises what He cannot do. Give, and it shall be given to you. Personally, I have a principle that every time I receive a blessing from whichever source, I must make sure I bless somebody in return. This way I have seen God open doors of blessings, even those I never expected or imagine. Giving brings a divine spiritual breakthrough because you practice God's character of giving. He is a giver. Do you resemble God in your giving? Whom do you resemble by being mean? As you answer this question, you can make an about-turn and start giving, and your life will never be the same anymore.

Jonah was given a message for the Ninevites, but he tried to use his common sense. He landed in a trance that fixed him so tight that he had to go to the initial God-planned destination because God isn't a man that He should change. Even today God hasn't changed; He is the same yesterday, today, and forevermore. Every time you are given something, the trend of God is that you give, and in return, you get. The circle continues, but many break the giving circuit by using their common sense, which is dominated by greed.

Fear not as you give, and it will be well with you both spiritually and physically. As you develop this God-given character, you will realize that it's so easy to serve God in any other way because the initial step is well cared for. It's from here that you will feel persuaded to keenly note that even serving, preaching, singing, and so forth aren't effective until they cost you something.

Lake Victoria is a freshwater lake. The River Nile, which benefits many people in the African countries, flows from this lake. Because it has an outlet, it has flesh water fit for human consumption. The Dead Sea, on the contrary, has no outlet, and its water is unfit for human consumption, unlike Lake Victoria. Nothing comes out of it, and hence it has no benefits to human beings. With these two examples, I hope you can now comprehend how nice and blessed it is to give than to receive, even as the Bible clearly states.

As you practice giving, you create room for more, and you become a continuous recipient as you continue to distribute, and the circuit proceeds as God intends it to. By giving I mean giving all things and in all areas. For example, if you receive a blessing sermon in your church, make sure you share it with somebody else, and you will soon realize that as you share, the message sticks so much in you that it becomes part and parcel of you. If you are promoted at your place of work, promote those under you, even if it's the servant boy and you will experience peace, joy, and more blessings as the one you promote must remember you in his or her prayers. If your samba or farm yields much harvest, make a point of visiting one who isn't privileged with a samba. As you visit this person, carry some of the harvest to him or her, and you will add to the number of your friends and intercessors in appreciation of your doing good.

If you start milking, sacrifice a bottle or two in obedience to God's word in favor of somebody who doesn't have a cow; and as he or she enjoys that tea the person makes with your gift, he or she must remember to thank God for you and so forth.

Many rivers flow to the Dead Sea, and instead of it supplying other dry areas around it, it just sits. Therefore rotting occurs that doesn't benefit anybody, and this brings its death name. Lake Victoria receives water from those rivers, and in return, it creates room for more as it flows out the River Nile to other people. Both the river and the lake are beneficial to many people, even fish.

Others will enjoy our lives as we become a blessing to them in obedience to the word of God by giving as we receive. Are you like Lake Victoria or the Dead Sea? It's never too late if you have been like the Dead Sea. If you have been like Lake Victoria, just keep it up and never give up, for there is no loss in giving like there is when we withhold what we have freely received from God.

Therefore, fear not as you give, because you will always be on the safe side. Never be tired of doing good as you serve God, because even brother Paul encouraged us, "Therefore, my beloved brethren, be ye immovable always abiding in the work of the Lord, for as much as ye know that your labor is not in vain in the Lord" (1 Corinthians 15:58).

Other points I feel persuaded to stress further—in addition to the fact that giving isn't giving until it cost you something—are the following: Serving isn't serving until it costs you something. Preaching isn't preaching until it cost you something. Singing isn't singing until it costs you something. Anointing isn't anointing until it costs you something. Leaving isn't leaving until it costs you something. Working isn't working until it costs you something.

Let me endeavor to elaborate further on each of the above points so we can better comprehend them.

## Serving Isn't Serving until It Costs You Something

Serving God is very costly, and no wonder many people don't like it. To some extent, it can even cost you your friends, relatives, wife, children, parents, jobs, health, even your own life and so forth. We have witnessed cases either of ourselves or of our very close friends who have been fired from jobs just because of serving God or even professing Christ as their Lord and Savior. Others have been deserted by friends just because of serving God. Others have been forsaken by their beloved spouses as those spouses give devil-inspired excuses that their loved ones are always out on missions or overnight prayer meetings and rarely have time for them. Some have been disowned by their own parents just because of the gospel. This is what I mean by service that costs you something. If you happen to be a victim of one of these experiences, take heart because God sees and understands, and our crowns in heaven are still being beautified every time we lose something worldly for God's service because he is faithful.

My encouragement to you, dear friend, is this. Right where you are, maybe you have been mistreated for the sake of the Lord many times. Please take heart and don't give up. The Lord understands, and He will see you through. Even as is the theme of this book, fear not. He will never leave you or forsake you.

## Preaching Isn't Preaching Until It Costs You Something

Preaching that is effective and anointed must cost a preacher, including his sweat as he prays in preparation for the sermon, several meals (if not one) as he fasts over the same, time as he goes through the Bible and searches for various scriptures applicable to the message as the Holy Spirit guides him, and the company and warmth of dear friends as he isolates himself in search of God's sanctification and use. Such a sermon for sure must bring sinners to repentance, the sick to health, the discouraged to encouragement, fear to boldness, and so forth. On the other hand, you can still get preaching that hasn't cost the preacher anything, and the results will be well manifested in the boredom, dozing, yawning, noise, stretching of arms as the congregation look at their watches, comings and goings of different people like they are in a recreation theater, and so forth. Does your preaching cost you something? If not, then I am sure it doesn't yield anything but only fulfills religious routines and duties. Costly preaching is always prolific for the glory of God.

Singing isn't singing until it costs you something; as mentioned earlier, I am a gospel singer, so I personally know what it means and costs as you sing for God. This price includes suspicions from the outside world that you are in business to make money, hatred as your close friends say you are proud because of your gift of singing, your time and meditation over scriptures as you compose songs, and much prayer over given tunes, which the devil always like snatching. You soon forget after you compose a song that you really need to be in the presence of God in prayer to avoid many voices that can easily take the glory of God.

God will never share His glory with any man. This truth is very common in the world we are in, and that is why some anointed singers lose their vision and end up like the foolish Galatians, beginning in the Spirit and ending up in the flesh. "O foolish Galatians who hath bewitched you, that ye should not obey the truth, before whose eyes Jesus Christ hath been evidently set forth, crucified among you? Are you so foolish? having began in the spirit, are ye now made perfect by the flesh?" (Galatians 3:1, 3). Singing can cost us shame at times, and even in this situation, we have to listen to God keenly as He tells us, "Fear not."

Once, different congregations, not my home church, invited me to minister in singing at two different crusades. As at other times, I prayed about the crusades, and I was convinced that I should attend only one of them since they were on the same date. I was to minister for two consecutive days. On the first day, I ministered. After I left the pulpit, the leader of that particular session made an announcement that anybody wishing to sing should specifically use the national languages, not the vernacular, and my songs were in the vernacular. I never thought I was to be a victim the following day, since they had officially invited me long before the crusade, and I had replied to their letter in acceptance of the invitation. I had also lucidly indicated that my songs were in vernacular.

After the crusade was over, I requested to minister the following day in the morning session, which was a Sunday because schools were opening the following Monday. As a mother, I needed to prepare my children for school. The request was granted, and I was grateful to God.

Reaching home, I met my son, who had a fever and an irritating cough. I knew the devil was out to disrupt my service for God, and I prayed, determined to be at the crusade at the expected time. We consented with my dear husband, who has always been an encouragement as I serve God, that he would be left with our son so I could go to the crusade. I went with my daughter and house girl to the crusade. Married women will agree with me that it takes the hand of the almighty God for a man and especially an African to consent to do some duties, and that is why I don't take it for granted that I can even get permission. You cannot effectively serve God without the consent of your husband, and I thank God continually for my husband.

On Sunday, we left for the crusade, and I reported to the organizer on arrival, who assured me that all was well and that I should be ready because I was to be summoned to sing in the first session. The time came, but the session leader said, "There is a girl called Florence who had requested to sing. Let her come quickly." I hesitated for two reasons: First, I wasn't a girl but a married woman, and my CD, which he held, lucidly indicated my name preceded by a "Mrs." Second, I hadn't requested a chance to sing, but they had officially invited me to minister in singing, and I heeded their invitation.

Because of these two good reasons, I delayed, but seeing no other girl going to the front, I woke up and ran to the platform to confirm. The crusade was well attended, since it was the final day, and people stared at me from all sides. Just before I held the microphone to begin singing, I was asked whether I would be singing Kikuyu or Kiswahili, and when I said Kikuyu, I was dismissed out of hand. I was so embarrassed in front of such a big congregation that I wished the earth could just open up and swallow me like in the time of Dathan and Korah in the Bible. I went back to my seat, and everybody gazed at me like I was a cartoon character as they wondered what had transpired at the platform. Tears welled up in my eyes, but I pleaded with God not to allow a single drop, especially in the company of my little daughter and my house girl.

My daughter quickly asked me, "Mum, why didn't you sing?" I wisely told her I would sing later in the afternoon, and she asked whether she could accompany me to sing, and I told her yes. My house girl also asked me, but I ignored her with, "There is no problem. I will sing later." My God-given humanity was very active, and I was there physically, but my mind hovered in many directions as I regretted why I had left my sick child at home in the name of serving God. The situation ended up in total frustrations. I wondered whether I would ever continue singing for God again, and I tell you it wasn't easy.

One of the ushers came to console me, but her comfort brought more harm than good because I felt so bitter. I couldn't comprehend why they had just resorted to shame me in such a place. Being it was the final day of the crusade, everybody who had missed the other days had availed himself or herself to be in attendance at that time. I wished time and again that the embarrassing event could have occurred on the previous day at least, when there weren't many people there, including my daughter. It was such a humiliating situation.

I proceeded to blame God and ask why He had allowed such a thing to happen to His servant. At that time, I remembered my Savior Jesus bearing all the shame and scoffing rude for my sake at the cross of Calvary. We also have to follow Him in all He passed through. I was encouraged deep within. His experience was so applicable to me, and I held on to Him. Isaiah 43:1–2 was also of great assistance. The Holy Spirit reminded me as I sat on that seat that I will always remember that date. Therefore, with the word dwelling richly in you, the Holy Spirit will always quicken them at the hour of need when we cannot even manage to take a Bible and literally read it. Fear not because God is with you. In whatever situation you are in, God is telling you, "Fear not, I am with you. You are mine." In that shame, He was with me, and I knew it was very costly serving God, even in singing.

## Anointing Isn't Anointing until It Costs You Something

God's anointing doesn't just come; one must be before God for some time in humility and self-denial, praying, fasting, being in isolation, and so forth. We see that Jesus, the Son of God, was anointed when He fasted for forty days and forty nights in the wilderness. You have to be in a wilderness of some kind, be it spiritual or physical; but a wilderness has to be there. Your being anointed may even cause death threats, such as those Joseph received. Joseph was very young when he was anointed at the age of seventeen, which in our country isn't a mature age according to the government. This fact gives me courage that our age is immaterial to God as long as we are able to comprehend obeying Him and walking in His ways. Joseph began having revelations from God through dreams.

> And Joseph brought unto his father their evil report, now Israel loved Joseph more than all his children because he was the son of his old age, and he made him a coat of many colors. And when his brothers saw that their father loved him more than all his brethren, they hated him and could not speak peaceable unto him. And Joseph dreamed a dream, and he told it to his brethren and they hated him yet the more. And he said unto them. Hear, I pray you this dream which I have dreamed. For behold, we were binding sheaves in the field and lo, my sheaf rose, and also stood upright, and behold, your sheaves stood around about, and made their obeisance to my sheaf. And his brethren said to him, 'shalt thou indeed have dominion over us?' And they hated him yet the more for his dreams and for his words. And he dreamed yet another dream and told it to his brethren and said, behold I have dreamed a dream more, and behold, the sun and the moon and the eleven stars make obeisance to me. And he told it to his father and to his brethren and his father rebuked him and said unto him, what is this dream that thou has dreamed? Shall I and thy mother and thy brethren indeed come to bow down ourselves

## Fear Not; God Is in Charge

to thee to the earth? And his brothers envied him; but his father observed the saying. (Genesis 37:2–11)

From these scriptures, we find that Joseph was living a life of truth since he couldn't hide from his father the evil deeds of his brethren when they were away, looking after their flock. He "brought unto his father their evil report." We must walk in truth if any anointing will ever come upon our lives. We need to expose every kind of evil in our environment, no matter how painful it may be. They weren't happy with him for reporting them. You know when you expose brethren of their evil deeds; hatred will obviously come.

I thank God for this young boy, who didn't mind the outcome of his stand in truth. Many times we fail to accomplish God's will in our lives because of endeavoring to see ahead of God; we are mindful of the future or the outcome of our taking a step in a particular thing, which is right in God's eyes but displeasing to our dear ones. It was after exposing the evil deeds that God began revealing spiritual things of the future to Joseph through dreams. Personally, I have witnessed that it's when I completely surrender to God and release my whole being that He reveals things to me. As in the case of this young Joseph, first evil had to be exposed before the revelations came. The hatred continued to accelerate as God continued to use him. It's good to be aware that when we fully surrender ourselves to God for His use, we declare war on the enemy, who will use every available chance through anybody to vigorously fight our service for God.

One evening after work, I received a message that a certain lady I didn't know wanted to see me, and I followed the directions she gave to her place. She had a spiritual need. Her seven-year-old boy had disappeared from home to an unknown destination, and she needed prayers. She wasn't saved, but I admonished her to be in prayers and fasting the following day. I informed one of my prayer partners, and the three of us purposed to be in prayers the following day.

In the evening, I passed through her place as agreed with the others because I had left work late so we could wind up the prayers together. A miracle had happened. The night before, the mother of the lost kid had felt inspired and persuaded to go to her maternal home, which was in another district, to check for the boy. Humanity in her had previously ruled out the idea because the boy seemed too small to go by himself, but praise God because when prayers were offered, the Holy Spirit imparted an idea in her. Believe it or not, the boy had traveled all the way to his grandmother's place, an event that shocked many. God was looking for an opportunity to save the parents. As we shared hilariously, both parents accepted the Lord as their Savior. One night at the same hour, two souls were snatched from the enemy for heaven. Their hearts had already been nourished with the word of God, which ended up bringing fruits of salvation. I led them in the prayer of repentance, and it was wonderful. What a mighty God we serve, who is able to glorify Himself through thick-and-thin circumstances because He is Jehovah and never respects personalities. As we parted, the wonderful intervention of our able God overwhelmed our hearts.

When I reached home, my son was very sick and wheezing. At once, I realized it was an attack of the enemy, who was furious that two souls had left him for the kingdom of God. A brother in Christ had come to see us, and I told him to lay hands on my son, and we prayed because the enemy wasn't impressed with the good work accomplished for the Lord. After thirty minutes, the boy was okay, and he ate supper, which he hadn't managed to do earlier due to his health status.

The point I want to put across to your heart is that as you serve God, be careful because the enemy always looks for an opportunity to attack to dispirit you. All the same, we are always winners with Christ, and the devil must be subdued in Jesus's name. Be alert and be fully equipped with the full armor of God to fight Him when He confronts you. Our always-available armor in Ephesians 6 is enough, and of course in combination with the other ammunition from Genesis to Revelation, it is enough to give us the needed victory over our foe.

One of our branch church pastors was preaching during a Sunday service from Ephesians 4:1–14 on the gifts of the Holy Spirit. He stressed the importance of the gifts of the Holy Spirit to every believer and said that each believer has one gift for the benefit of the body of Christ. I liked the way he narrated the episode through the revelation of the Holy Spirit as he compared the Ephesian church to Christians today. The Ephesian church was powerful but also miserable because they had all they needed spiritually, but they were like poor shoppers. As Christians, spiritual blessings are like a full supermarket, and Christ paid the bill on Calvary when He said, "All is finished." Unfortunately, some Christians are like the poor shoppers of Ephesians, not knowing they have all they need in Christ. These Ephesians left without buying anything, yet all had been paid for them.

After preaching, the pastor had a last session of praying for ministries for those who so desired it after the service was over. I was left behind, and as I prepared to go in front to be prayed for, I pleaded to God to know what I was supposed to be doing in the body of Christ pertaining to the sermon he had preached. When he laid his hands on me, I also began praying silently to God. He actually took time with me, and God gave him a word of knowledge for me. It was this way: "As I called you to work for Me, I will continue to be with you. The field is still big. I will bless your family, and don't rely on your income. Look unto Me, the Lord, who has called you."

I cried openly to God in front there as I remembered the prophecy of the previous time eight months ago. Note the similarity of these two messages from God at different times by different people of different congregation and in different ways.

> July 21, 1996: As I called Abraham out of his clan, so am I calling you to bless you and to bless nations through you. I will give. I will give you what to take where I send you.

> March 23, 1997: As I called you to work for Me, I will continue to be with you. The field is still big. I will bless your family, and don't rely on your income. Look unto Me, the Lord, who has called you.

When we fully surrender ourselves to God in humility, He creates chances of anointing us for His own glory, and the anointing many times comes when we don't even think we are anointed because of the surrounding circumstances. With the anointing of God, all will be provided for us in this journey because Jehovah Jireh is in control. Anointing brings blessings. Abraham was anointed of God, and hence other nations were blessed through him. He was obedient to God. Without obedience to our master, we cannot experience the divine anointing.

Joseph was anointed of God, and so he became a blessing to his entire household in the time of famine. The anointing gives no place for revenge against your enemies, and no wonder Joseph encouraged his brothers to take heart when they felt guilty about what they had done to him. "Now therefore, be not grieved, nor angry with yourselves, thy ye sold me hither: for God did send me before you to preserve life" (Genesis 45:5). When you are under the anointing of God, you take all things for the glory of God, either bad or good. Though his brothers meant evil against him when they sold him, God worked out a good plan for all of them. The anointing cost Joseph's humiliation, but his entire household enjoyed the end result.

"Behold we were binding sheaves in the field and lo my sheaf rose, and also stood upright, and behold, your sheaves stood round about and made obeisance to my sheaf" (v. 7). This was nothing but the truth Joseph received from the Lord, and he sincerely told his brethren the same truth without hiding it since his heart was clean, unlike theirs. He was under anointing, but his brothers were under the influence of a superiority complex syndrome.

Those not under the anointing will hate and envy those who have the anointing. So get ready, my friend, if you are anointed; you will be hated, but give praise to God because the anointing will always provide everything you need. The Bible tells us that many are the afflictions of the righteous, but the Lord delivers him from *all* of them and not *some*. Amen. "Many are the afflictions of the righteous: but the Lord delivereth him out of them all" (Psalm 34:19).

"Shalt thou indeed reign over us?" or "Shalt thou indeed have

## Fear Not; God Is in Charge

dominion over us?" These are two questions full of jealousy, fear of being ruled by a younger brother, forgetting that age and status are immaterial before God, who isn't a respecter of persons. Even today, many people, even Christians, are so power hungry that they had better miss the visitation and blessings of God than be ruled by one they consider inferior to them, no matter how anointed of God he or she may be. This is hazardous, and unless we get a second touch, the devil, who is always informed of everything, will use this chance to prevent God from using many.

Never give the devil a chance. Their position in the family blinded these brothers of Joseph; they thought they couldn't be in a position to enjoy God's presence as He used their younger brother. You know even today the devil is using many things in our lives to be barriers so we don't see God as He visits us—for example, pride, riches, age, family background, education status, positions in our places of work, tribalism, and so forth. I urge every reader of this book to be conscious of these worldly, temporal things.

This message also reminds me of the importance of worship to our God. Some people are so conscious of their personalities that they cannot worship God as God Himself expects them or the Holy Spirit convicts them. Worship is giving all of ourselves and all we have in appreciation to your maker. You know worship in its real meaning can make us cry forever before God (worth ship of our God), but the enemy knows that there is a great anointing in worship, and so he comes when you raise your hands, worshipping God, and reminds you that you are a boss; and your juniors will discredit you if they see a full managing director or whichever title you have. Forget about yourself and concentrate on God when you go before Him, regardless of your position. Kneel before Him if you feel He is worth that. Cry if you feel He is worth your tears. Laugh, clap, shout, scream, and so forth. For sure you cannot leave that place without the anointing of God.

"And he dreamed yet another dream and told it to is brethren and said, behold I have dreamed a dream more; and behold the sun and the moon and the eleven stars made obeisance to me" (v. 9). As at other times, because he was heavily anointed, he continued to tell the truth, not knowing the effects on the hearers. When a man of God is heavily anointed, he talks under that anointing, not knowing the effects on his listeners. Some are usually very happy, but others are hurt. This is very common, even as it was with the birth of Jesus. Some were happy, and others like Herod were troubled. "When Herod the King heard these things, he was troubled and all Jerusalem with him" (Matthew 1:3). Why was Herod troubled? He had heard that a king had been born and wondered what would become of himself as king. He was power hungry, as mentioned earlier. He couldn't imagine being overthrown from his post of being a king.

Even today, things haven't changed. When a member of a particular church is more anointed than the leaders, battles against him or her arises because they fret this upcoming anointed brother or sister will soon take over in leadership. This is a very bad spirit, which is eating the body of Christ badly. Jesus encountered such a congregation and concluded that whosoever wishes to be great in the kingdom of God should be the servant of the others, and He literally washed the feet of His disciples as a good example. May God help us to know that to be great in the kingdom of God, we need to be servants of God and His workmen.

It isn't until we realize that Jesus is like the doctor and we are like the nurses that we shall have breakthroughs in our homes, marriages, churches, offices, and so forth. The doctor does the main surgical or treatment works, and the nurses assist as they carry the necessary tools for the particular operation for him wherever he goes. If it is a file of a patient, the nurse takes it to the doctor; a bandage she also takes and all that is required, but a nurse can never operate on a patient. May the Holy Spirit of God help us know that we are there as servants to carry tools for our doctor, Jesus, to do the operation in the hearts of sinful, sick, possessed, discouraged people. You could be carrying the bandage to put on that wound the devil has put on a person, and I will be carrying the injection medicines. Another nurse may carry theater kits and so forth. But we all serve one doctor, Jesus. Ours is just to obey what Christ tells us, and He will do the work through us.

## Fear Not; God Is in Charge

We are the mouths of God to speak on what we have been sent to do and legs to go where the gospel is needed.

When you are under anointing, you say nothing but the truth like Joseph did when he told his second dream. Joseph continued with the excitement of the anointing and told his father of the dream. "And he told it to his father and to his brethren and *his father rebuked him* and said unto him, what is this dream that thou hast dreamed?" (v. 10, emphasis added). Imagine his own father, who loved him more than all his other sons, now rebuking him—not because Joseph had stopped obeying him but because he had told him the plain truth of his revelation from God through the dream. Mind you, the dream wasn't his own making, but God revealed it to him. Today do you know that as many continue in the anointing, the number of their enemies continues to increase? Even their very close friends leave, believing there is pretense of revelation, pride, self-exaltation, and so forth. I mean friends like in the case of Joseph—fathers, mothers, wives, husbands, your so-called partners, next of kin, and so forth. But the truth must be told if it is God who has called us to turn from all works of darkness. Joseph's father wondered and asked his son plainly, "Shall I and thy mother and thy brethren indeed come to bow down ourselves to thee to the earth?"

The father under all circumstances couldn't comprehend how he as his father who bore him could kneel before Joseph. He even wondered, on behalf of his wife who was the mother of Joseph, how a woman who had carried him for nine good months during pregnancy and weaned him, letting him suck her breasts, could also kneel before him. Surely he reminded Joseph of what the Law of Moses said. "Honor thy father and mother for this is the first commandment with a promise." He must have warned him to stop those nonsensical dreams lest he be cursed for failing to honor his parents. What a mighty God we serve who isn't bothered with our position in families when He wants to use us for His glory as long as we are available and yielded to Him. His ways are not like our ways, because as the heavens are far from the earth, so are the ways of the Lord. His requirements are simple: availability, willingness and humility and all you need is to say is, 'Here I am, Lord, use me'.

That is enough qualification before God. He is always looking for an available vessel, even as He asked Isaiah, "Whom shall I send?" He never asked for a prominent or qualified vessel but one that was available. Amen. Are you available now? Are you willing? Are you going to yield yourself to Him? These are the only questions you need to answer, and you will be ready to be used of God, and His anointing will be upon you, and you will do exploits for Him. That is the price of bearing the anointing of God.

When you are under the anointing of God, you don't need to struggle like you are alone. God will always open doors in His own ways because He is Jehovah Jireh. If ever you happen to see a servant of God struggling, then the person must be trying to serve God by his or her own might, and no wonder the Bible clearly states that it's "not by power or might" as referenced in Zachariah. 4:6 but by the Spirit of the Lord. The anointing will always provide all things.

## Leaving Isn't Leaving until It Costs You Something

Adam and Eve did the first leaving in the Garden of Eden. They left the presence of God, where He wanted them to stay in peace but because of disobedience, it costed them their rest since God vowed that a man had to eat out of his own sweat. It cost them a good thing, but for this case, I would like us to focus on leaving bad things to attain good ones in Jesus's name. In marriage, a man has to leave his parents to be joined to his wife, which is a blessing when we obey God as He directs. A lady leaves her parents, whom she has stayed with for many years since birth, when she marries. It isn't very easy to leave, adapting to a new life, but then she must do it to obey God, which brings blessings. I have been married for many years, and I still have some things I haven't adapted to completely on the other side in my marital life. So what I mean is that leaving is very dear. When we get saved, we are expected to leave our old sinful natures, which cost us many pleasures of this world, and even allies who used to be very close to us; but for the sake of our heavenly journey, we purpose to leave them. These are allies we used to match nicely for the sake of our knowing Christ due to some sinful behaviors we cannot cope with. You forsake good businesses that are corrupt despite their booming rate for the sake of obeying the word, even as brother Paul says,

> Be ye not unequally yoked together with unbelievers for what fellowship hath righteousness with unrighteousness? and what communion hath light with darkness? And what concord hath Christ with Beliah? or what part hath he that believeth with an infidel? And what agreement hath the temple of God with idols? For ye are the temple of the living God; as God hath said, I will dwell in them, and walk with Them; and I will be their God, and they shall be my people. wherefore come out from among them, and be ye separate, saith the Lord, and touch not the unclean thing; and I will receive you. And will be a Father unto you, and ye shall be my sons and daughters, saith the Lord Almighty. (2 Corinthians 7:14–18)

From this text, we clearly see that we belonged somewhere before we invited Christ into our hearts, and a separation is mandatory to have God as our Father; we are also to be sons and daughters to the almighty God. Having fellowship with Christ costs us our friends. We also note that truth before we were in darkness, and forsaking the same for righteousness is also mandatory and expensive too. We were in darkness and now have entered light, which are two different things, and it's not easy to leave one for the sake of the other. We may have been in agreement with idols but now we are the temples of God. So we have to completely wipe away all we had with idols, like witch doctors, for the holy God to rule our lives. Such surrender is costly. We were so much in the worldly things and people, and we are being commanded to *come out* from among them and *be separate*, and so it is costly too. We have heard cases in the medical circle where two or three children are born while sharing the same heart. It isn't an easy operation, and at times not all the lives of the kids are spared. It is a hard and complicated operation, and in the same way, it is hard to separate ourselves, but it is worth it when we choose to obey our maker. Therefore, leaving our old nature will cost us many things we used to value, but it is rewarding when we do it in obedience to our God.

## Working Isn't Working until It Costs Us Something

At least every worker well comprehends this one, be it in offices, homes, businesses, and so forth. since most people work in different fields. Work generally costs us many things—for example, sweet sleep, since we need to wake up early in the morning, especially on a chilly, drizzling day, if we expect our daily pay. For a farmer, work has to cost him his sweat when digging, money for the seedlings and fertilizer, laborers for a good harvest, and also time of waiting.

In the spiritual realm, work costs us time as we labor for God, our strength as we walk long distances when in missions or going for fellowships, our money as we give cheerfully toward the work of God, and many other things we may also know of yourself. It costs us to work for the Lord, but our joy is that we are paid in this present time, and for the time to come, life everlasting is awaiting us. So it isn't in vain that we serve the Lord, and Paul encourages us today the way he encouraged the Corinthians. "Therefore, my beloved brethren, be ye steadfast, unmovable, always abounding in the work of the Lord, forasmuch as ye know that your labor is not in vain in the Lord" (1 Corinthians 15:58). Now we see how working, be it spiritual or physical, costs many things, but glory be to God because it isn't in vain we are losing in this world for the heavenly kingdom's sake. God is never tired of giving us all things, including forgiveness; and as our heavenly Father, if we emulate Him, we have nothing to lose anyway.

A farmer who expects a good harvest labors to till the land,

## Fear Not; God Is in Charge

plants seeds, and waits for germination. While patiently waiting, he continues to attend to the grown crops till they are harvested. Harvest time bring joy, which never automatically comes while he relaxes. No way. I bet inner relaxing is there, but physical labor is mandatory for any fruits, which are always nice to see and healthy to our bodies. The kingdom of God can never tolerate lazybones or couch potatoes. Remember, you have something to do no matter where you are, who you are, or who knows you. First and foremost, recognize your identity in Christ to manage and face life without fear. Excuses in the kingdom of God aren't welcome, but initiatives are encouraged; and once God sees you've taken a step to do something, He show up for you as a God of action, and His name is glorified. It's not about us but all for His glory. He is a jealous God who won't share His glory with any man. Amen.

## Chapter 5

# You and I Are Pilgrims on Earth

WE SHOULD NEVER entertain fear when we know we are but pilgrims in this world, looking for a city whose maker and builder is God. We are on transit to heaven, and that is enough reason to encourage us to fight every wind that blows through our lives to make us fret.

Looking deeply, we see that what a pilgrim means is worth it all so that the enemy doesn't hoodwink us like we are in this universe forever. There was a man in the time of Jesus who thought his riches would last forever, but Jesus called him a fool. May God help us not to be called fools by God as He looks at us and sees how we are so much entangled in this world, forgetting that soon and very soon we are going to our pilgrimage destination.

A pilgrim is a person who undertakes a journey to a sacred place as an act of religious devotion. Therefore, grammatically, everyone who professes Christ as Lord and Savior is a pilgrim. The Israelites were pilgrims from Egypt to the Promised Land of Canaan, which was flowing with milk and honey. Abraham was a pilgrim, a truth we see in Hebrews 11:8–10. "By faith Abraham when he was called to go Out into a place which he should after receive for an inheritance obeyed; and he went out, not knowing whither he went. By faith he sojourned in the land of promise as in a strange country, dwelling in tabernacles with Isaac and Jacob, the heirs with him of the same promise. He

## Fear Not; God Is in Charge

looked for a city which hath foundations, whose builder and maker is God." As we live in Christ, we are heading to a destination that is worth our patience and perseverance. It isn't in vain because we will be like Jesus and live with Him forever when we finish this journey faithfully. Do you feel like it's too much to bear? Take heart; we are heading to our eternal destination.

The Kamba people (a tribe in Kenya) are normally used to trekking long distances, and if you happen to accompany them for the first time, you will be surprised because if you get tired and ask whether you are near your destination, they will say, "No vaa, no vaa," meaning it's just near here. Wherever they say, "No vaa" may be many kilometers from the destination. I believe this is what Christians should encourage themselves in despite much heartache; here on earth we are soon leaving this world of fears and tumults. Hold on to your faith without wavering because "heaven no vaa," and you will rejoice when you reach there. Sorrows, pains, hatred, and all you feel you undergo unjustly will be no more.

Only praise and worship will be known there. Fear not, dear pilgrim, because our crowns in heaven are laid, ready, and waiting for us to finish this journey. The trial may cost us many things we value here on earth, but that joy will make us forget them all at once when we make it there. Normally what makes the physical journeys here cumbersome is the condition of the roads, which are full of potholes, but when we reach heaven, potholes will be tales to us. The roads are made of gold that shines more than electricity, power we have never seen on earth. No more school fees, water and electric bills, and the ever-increasing transport charges; we will rest forever. What a wonderful place is heaven. I long to be there. What about you, friend? Accept Christ to save you now, and you will be eligible for heaven.

Nevertheless, you and I as pilgrims must know that there are things every pilgrim must do:

1. Pilgrims must have faith.
2. Pilgrims must be determined to reach the destination.
3. Pilgrims must be ready to overcome.

## Pilgrims Must Have Faith

Faith, being the substance of things hoped for and the evidence of things not seen, provokes every pilgrim on his or her journey, having not seen heaven, to believe by faith (Hebrews 11). We must not go by what we see currently, but we should now act on our sixth common sense, without which we will only be meddling about in this life.

## Pilgrims Must Be Determined to Reach the Destination

Whenever determination is needed, there are always some hindering and opposing powers and situations. Therefore, we must be ready to overcome all these. The Israelites had opposition from the Egyptians, but their leader, Moses, kept encouraging them. Today, there are discouragements as we sojourn on this journey to heaven through sicknesses, criticism, lack of everyday needs as expected, and so forth, but thank God that Jesus Christ, His Son, is our leader; and because He overcame, we shall overcome as we look unto Him as the author and finisher of our faith. Following His footprints will be our key to victory, and we can easily locate these footprints in the word.

"God, who at sundry times and in divers manners spoke in the time past unto the fathers by the Prophets, hath in these last days spoken unto us by His son, whom He hath appointed heir of all things of his glory, and the express image of his person, and upholding all things by the word of his power, when he had by himself purged our sins sat down on the right hand of the majesty on high" (Hebrews 1:1–3 KJV).

We are very lucky since our leader, Christ, is more than a conqueror of all things death, temptations, false accusations, and so forth. Therefore, if we follow in His footsteps, we shall surely be like Him. All that would not make us conquerors like Him is failing to follow His footsteps. He prayed and fasted, and we must do the same to attain the victory over the evil one as He did. He read the word thoroughly, and no wonder He replied to the devil, "It is written"

## Fear Not; God Is in Charge

when Satan tempted Him various times after He had finished forty days and forty nights of praying and fasting.

He loved people without partiality, unlike us today who always regard personalities. He preached the good news of the kingdom, and so must we. He comforted the lonely and healed the sick. and the list is endless of the many good things He did; so should our list of good things be endless if we expect to be conquerors. The holy word of God is also our guide. "Thy word is a lamp unto my feet, and a light unto my path (Psalm 119:105). David was a king, but he knew that without the word to guide him, he couldn't manage.

No matter your status, you need the word because it will be your guide on the way. No position or status can replace the work of God's word in our lives if we are to live godly. Forget about your status now and lean not on your own comprehension but on the word of God, which will guide and lead you well.

As pilgrims, at times the road becomes dark and hence needs the word as a light. The Holy Spirit is also our guide and counselor, even as we see what Jesus prayed for us.

Jesus Himself promised His disciples, of whom we are today, "And I will pray the Father and He shall give you another comforter, that He may abide with you forever. Even the Spirit of truth; whom the world cannot receive, because it seeth him not, neither knoweth him; but you know him; for he dwelleth with you and shall be in you. I will not leave you comfortless: I will come to you" (John 14:16–18). Jesus is still encouraging us the way He did the disciples; therefore, we need to trust and obey all He tells us to do in the holy word. Without the word, we are bound to struggle in vain. The Holy Spirit in us acts like a catalyst, making easy things that seem so hard to us. Once He is in us, things will be okay; otherwise without Him, we will be struggling the way manual-driven machine operators struggle unlike the automatic-driven machines.

I have done typing, and it's so tedious using a manual typewriter unlike the electric ones, which are so soft as I touch the keys. The completed job of an electric typewriter is appealing because even erasing is done automatically. On the other hand, a manually erased work is normally untidy. The Holy Spirit makes our spiritual lives manageable, and I would urge every Christian to desire to be filled daily. He assists us in managing this spiritual life without much struggle, but then we must be ready to invite Him to guide us. As said many times in this book, you have your part to play, and God has His. God always acts when we take an action. Idleness and ignorance are enough to make you a total failure in the things of God

## Fellowship of Other Pilgrims

"Take heed, brethren lest there be in any of you an evil heart of unbelief, in departing from the living God, but exhort one another daily; while it is called today; lest any of you be hardened through deceitfulness of sins" (Hebrews 3:12–13). Somebody shared and said, "Christians are fellows in a ship heading to one common destination," bringing in the word *fellowship*. We need to be together, sharing our common goals and experiences in this heavenly journey as we see the days drawing near than when we first believed for encouragement purposes. "No temptation has taken you but such as is common to man; but God is faithful who will not suffer you to be tempted above that ye are able; but will with the temptation also make a way to escape, that ye may be able to bear it" (1 Corinthians 10:13).

From this scripture, the idea of isolation is discouraged because if you are alone and problems come, you will always speculate that nobody can ever experience a thing like yours and afford a smile. Then the devil makes you believe you are hopeless only because you lost a job or something of the sort the other day. If you go to a fellowship and brothers or sisters share how one time they lost their job, the shamba was auctioned, the kids were sick, and God was still faithful, you get encouraged and know surely your losing a job was a very minor problem.

The main reason the devil discourages us from fellowships is for his own discouraging tactics. "Not forsaking the assembling of ourselves together, as the manner of some is: but exhorting one another; and so much the more, as ye see the day approaching" (Hebrews 10:25). God's word is very specific and true; from these scriptures note "as the manner of some is." For sure many of us forsake fellowships, and we fail to understand whether they aren't prone to the devil's traps. Wake up, my fellow pilgrim, and regard fellowship. You will agree with me that the coming of our Lord Jesus Christ is much nearer than when we first believed, even as our quotation states.

Therefore, we need fellowships more than when we first believed. It's very surprising because the whole thing is vice versa. When we got saved, we were more zealous for God than now. Watch out! Things are taking the wrong course. It's now that we should be more zealous because the day is very near, just like the twinkling of an eye, and the Son of Man will be revealed. If you put charcoal in a *jiko* (an African stove) and light a fire, it will be very hard to put the fire out at once. I have many times watched charcoal in a *jiko*, and if there's not enough to cover all the holes, the fire definitely won't light.

The more charcoal you use determines the strength of the fire for what you need it for. Again, if you want to extinguish this fire when it is nicely burning, my friend, you cannot just put it out all at once; you will need to sprinkle water bit by bit to extinguish all the fire. This phenomenon is very applicable in our spiritual lives. In a very large fellowship, the Holy Ghost fire burns, and the devil isn't able to move you, though he will try anyway since that is his work of trial and error on Christians. It's in this fellowship that you will attain spiritual warmth to carry you through when you are alone as you ponder various testimonies and work in the aforetime fellowship. You will sort of be chewing cud and hence be able to overcome that challenge at that particular time. When the enemy confronts you, have a good treasure of spiritual materials in your life, and you will manage with the Lord.

Friends, we need not be ignorant of Satan's devices because he is powerful, and so we also need to be powerful in the Lord and in the power of His might to fight this enemy of the cross. Be ready to fight with the devil, but glory be to God because our victory over him is already there but on condition that we obey what God tell us in His holy word. We are fighting an already-won battle by Christ since that time He said, "It is finished."

Start isolating yourself bit by bit from the large fellowships to one or two brothers' fellowships, and finally you are all alone as you embark, claiming they are offending you. The devil being on the rampage will work on you properly, and finally you are no more to be called a brother or sister. The same devil then starts encouraging you to say, "If it were not for so-and-so, I would not have left the Lord." Come on, friend! "Let us hold fast the profession of our faith without wavering; (for he is faithful that promised)" (Hebrews 10:23). God has promised He will never leave us or forsake us. That is not a friend, mother, or father; but *God has promised*, and His promises are yea and amen, and He never promises what He cannot fulfill.

"Looking unto Jesus the author and finisher of our faith; who for the joy that was set before him endured the cross, despising the shame, and is set down at the right hand of the throne of God" (Hebrews 12:2). This means *looking unto Jesus*, not to anyone else, even if he is your breadwinner. Friends, let us stop looking to man with flesh and blood, but *look unto Jesus*, and we shall see the difference. For the crown of life awaiting us in heaven, be encouraged to look to this good Lord and shepherd. If Christ, the Son of God, endured the cross (and it wasn't easy at all), how much more do you speculate we need to endure the many hindrances we meet in this journey? It's not an easy road, but as we walk with the Lord, it will be easier for us; otherwise, by ourselves we will strive only in vain like trying to drive a car without fuel. It's impossible, my friend. Be fueled by the power of the Holy Ghost to manage this challenging journey, and after all our troubles are over, we shall tell the story of how we overcome when we reach home.

## Must Be Ready to Overcome

It's one thing to overcome and another to be ready to overcome. Since overcoming is to conquer, you must be having something else, which you are conquering. Surmounting is getting over; therefore, there must be something you are getting over. "Making powerless" means there is something powerful you want to defeat. In other words, You have a battle to overcome. I have seen people fight, and each person always endeavors to defeat his or her counterpart. There is always a resisting force from each person. We are being encouraged to resist the devil, and he will flee from us. The devil is our enemy, and we must be determined to overcome him. Like any fighting groups, the devil never gives up on his enemies until he sees them defeated. Why should you give up on him? Spectators are always eager to see the winner. Therefore, the devil, his demons, and all the enemies of the cross are eagerly waiting to see you defeated. On the other hand, the angels in heaven and all the friends of the cross are always cheering you up to overcome. The choice is yours. "Submit yourselves therefore to God. Resist the devil, and he will Flee from you. Draw near to God and he will draw nigh to you. Cleanse your hands, ye sinners; and purify your hearts, ye double minded" (James 4:7–8). From these scriptures, we see four conditions set for victory to be attained in the battle:

> 1. <u>Submitting</u>: There is a superior power we must submit ourselves to to win the battle (God's power). Our God is all powerful, so as we submit to Him, victory will be obvious.

> 2. <u>Resisting</u>: There is another power we must resist (devil's power). As we take the action of resisting, the devil will be on his heels, fleeing and not just running because of the superior working power of our mighty God. Amen.

> 3. <u>Drawing Near</u>: After resisting the devil and seeing him flee from us, we cannot just be in our normal position lest he comes back with more strength on us. We must draw near to our God, and He in return will

draw near to us and therefore give the devil a stronger blow by His presence.

4. <u>Cleansing:</u> To cleanse is to make pure. Since our God is holy, we must be holy also through the word for Him to use us. We cannot just expect God who is holy to use unholy vessels in a battle with the enemy. Normally when soldiers go out for battle, first they make sure they are fully armed for the battle lest they are defeated instantly. In the same way, we aren't different as we fight this good fight of faith. God has already prepared us a full armor to fight with. Our role is just to put on this armor.

Finally, my brethren, be strong in the Lord, and in the power Of his might. Put on the whole armor of God, that ye may be Able to stand against the wiles of the devil. For we wrestle Not against flesh and blood, but against principalities, against powers, against the rulers of the darkness of this World, against spiritual wickedness in high places. Wherefore Take unto you the whole armor of God that ye may be able to Withstand in the evil day, and having done all, to stand. Stand therefore, having your loins girt about with truth, and Having on the breastplate of righteousness; and your feet shod With the preparation of the gospel of peace; above all, Taking the shield of faith, wherewith ye shall be able to Quench all the fiery darts of the wicked. And take the helmet Of salvation, and the sword of the Spirit, this is the word Of God: "Praying always with all prayer and supplication in The Spirit, and watching thereunto with all perseverance and Supplication for all saints" (Ephesians 6:18).

## Fear Not; God Is in Charge

As we put on this *whole* armor of God, surely we shall overcome the enemy, but if we put on only part of the armor as many do, victory will be very hard. We are also to overcome because of the blood of Jesus and by the word of our testimony. "And they Testimony; and they loved not their lives unto the death" (Revelation 12:11). Our testimony is vital in this battle, even to the devil himself. We need to testify to the devil that we are saved by the blood of the lamb. Many have gotten another gospel of saying their deeds should testify, but my friend, be on the lookout. We need to say it with our mouths and combine it with deeds. Many have fallen prey to the enemy because of hiding their testimony as they await their fruits to show.

I am married, and during our time of courtship with my fiancé, who is now my husband, I was always happy to associate myself with him before accepting his proposal; at least I would not have publicly introduced him, not even to my parents, until we were fully committed. But after I said yes to his proposal, each of us confidently introduced ourselves to friends as "This is so-and-so, my fiancé" with a lot of joy and confidence. In the same manner, after we accept Christ as our personal Savior, we have accepted His proposal of being His. Amen. Therefore, every introduction of us should automatically be followed by Christ's position in our lives. Just imagine if I could have met a gentleman and my fiancé, and we cheerfully greeted each other; then off we left, the three of us, going out for coffee together with no introduction beyond saying, "Meet so-and-so." Obviously this situation would have created suspicion in my fiancé's mind or vice versa since it would mean to him that I was double-dealing him with that other man. What do you think the Lord Jesus feels when you meet a friend and say, "I am Florence," and that's all?

Who is God, and what does He mean in my life? I thank God that I am not ashamed of the gospel because it is power to me as a believer. Are you ashamed of associating yourself with the Lord Jesus everywhere, or is your testimony limited to places and people? Unless you are double-dealing in your Christian life in the things of darkness, surely I don't see any possibility of any Christian who is walking in the light being ashamed of the Lord's position in "his or her life". May God help us to give Christ His rightful position in our every introduction, because the Bible states clearly that they overcame by the *blood* and their *testimony*. Finally, let's remember we aren't in this world forever, but we are sojourners as we look for a city whose maker and builder is God. As pilgrims going to our predestined home (heaven), let us not be like Abraham and his father, Terah, who after reaching Haran on their way to Canaan thought they had reached it because of the many riches and the flourishing businesses they found there (Genesis 11:31). Their destiny was Canaan, but the devil blinded them with the riches and many good things in Harlan.

After begetting ourselves good things and attaining flourishing businesses, sorry to say that many are forsaking their faith and following riches. This world isn't our home, friends. Let us get out of this Harlan (world) and march to Canaan (heaven), our destination, whatever the cost, looking unto Jesus and not material things because He is the author and finisher of our faith. Going back to the original start can be detrimental to our spiritual lives. Imagine driving down a highway and seeing a driver ahead of you backing up. Whatever you imagine of that action, remember that forward to heaven have we been called, and backward never. If you chose to back up, there is danger not only to the one who initiated backing up but also impact to others on the highway. We are soldiers in the army of the Lord, marching to heaven, but we are still in this world, representing the heavenly kingdom. Backing up in our daily service or behavior affects others on the journey with us and prevents others from desiring the Christian life. Ambassadors of Christ we are, and by all means do we need to walk worthy of our calling without fear of any repercussions. With God all things are possible, even life, without compromising our integrity in Him. Many people around us haven't time to read the word of God or go to church, and they rely on us to reflect God.

# Chapter 6

# What the Bible Says about Fear

THE ENTIRE BIBLE in one way or another admonishes us to fight fear by trusting God for our lives. Normally, fear is brought by insecurity in life, such as security for our health, children or family members, respective nations, marriages, our future, and so forth. With all these fears, the Bible has a particular promise for each situation. The Bible, the inspired word of God, advises us to wholly depend on God's strength because carnal strength cannot go far. Our victory today over every kind of fear will depend on where we have put God in our lives. The word of God never supports fear; instead it is always against it. As said earlier in this book, from Genesis to Revelation, there are more than 365 or 366 "fear not"s. Similarly, there are 365 or 366 days in a year; therefore, there is enough provision of security from God each day as He tells you and me respectively, "Fear not." The only hassle is for the lazybones who never like reading the word, and hence they fail to know that in each day they face, be it good or bad, God is telling them, "Fear not." My challenge here is that every human being is expected by his creator to read the word. It was written purposely for our guidance. Many have endeavored to isolate themselves, but the word is for all human beings and not only for Christians. It is the word that talks to the sinner, calling him or her to repentance. This scripture is for an unbeliever, so read it and turn from your wickedness.

It is the one who has so many sins who is being called on to reason with God for cleansing. "Come now and let us reason together, saith the Lord: though your sins be as scarlet, they shall be as white as snow: though they be as red as crimson, they shall be as wool" (Isaiah 1:18). Here we clearly notice "your sins." So this person who is so sinful is being called. Therefore, the word is also for sinners to reason together with God for their cleansing. The troubled lot need the word even as Jesus reminds them, "Let not your heart be troubled: ye believe in God, believe also in me. In my father's house are many mansions. if it were not so, I would have told you. I go to prepare a place for you. And If I go and prepare a place for you, I will come again, and receive you unto myself; that where I am, there ye may be also. And whither I go ye know, and the way ye know" (John 14:1–4).

The disciples had known and walked with Jesus for a long time, and they sort of got used to Him and forgot His powers over every situation in their lives. As a result, they entertained fear that may have been due to what their eyes could realistically see around them. As earlier mentioned, reality and spiritual worlds are always parallel. A world of reality is a world that fights the spiritual world and believers who aren't well nourished with the word of God. Reality depends on seeing, while the spiritual world depends on faith. Therefore, we don't need to see to believe because we have faith. Reality will always insist on our seeing and hence go in the opposite direction from faith. Getting used to things in life brings reality. The way the disciples got used to being with Christ is the way many people today get used to the world and its things; the practices therein are a menace to the body of Christ. It is by getting used to Christianity in a worldly perspective that Christians today see there is nothing wrong in bribing, since they reason out that all others are doing it. Wake up if you are in that lot because we aren't *all others* or like *any other*.

The Bible clearly states that we are peculiar people. What does *peculiar* mean? Grammatically, it is defined with these words: *strange*, *particular*, or *belonging to*. We are strange people to the world and their behaviors, and there is no way we can entangle ourselves in the things they do if we read the word of God properly. Here I would like to assure every Bible reader and doer that God is God and not man. Obey what you read in the Bible because it is that word you read that will judge you. It doesn't matter whether others obey, but you obey since God deals with us individually. I have personally witnessed many times of individuality, especially when I go to church. A message comes through the sermon, a prophecy, a testimony, songs, and so forth. While I ponder my own life, the words in one of these ways speak directly and clearly to me. From that same service, later you hear that someone there personally declares that he or she was so bored that the person started sleeping in the middle of the sermon. Let us learn to listen, walk, obey, and so forth in an individual manner, and all will be well with our souls and our environs.

Being particular people is evidence that we need to behave particularly and not as others when we obey the word. We are either for God or not at all for God, but never can we be both for God and for the devil and claim to be walking in the word of God. A particular person for God can never join people doing evil because evil is done anyhow. The same words, if we read them well regularly and keenly, warn us against joining multitudes in doing evil. "Thou shalt not follow a multitude to do evil; neither shalt thou speak in a cause to decline after many to wrest judgment" (Exodus 23:2). A particular person will obey the word and be an intercessor of others instead of being just a talker of people, since the word clearly says, "I exhort therefore that first of all supplications, prayers, intercessions and giving of thanks be made for all men, for kings and for all that are in authority, that ye may lead a quiet and peaceable life in all godliness and honesty" (1 Timothy 2:1–2).

I thank God that His word is very systematic in all ways for all people. There is very good organization in the word of God, and this should give us the courage to read it always and obey it. Those who don't study the word are always disorganized, and hence confusion always arises in one way or another. Paul wrote this scripture to young Timothy, who was his spiritual child. He advised him of his rightful responsibility biblically. Many people these days are failing to take their rightful biblical responsibilities because they don't read the word, and if they do, it isn't dwelling richly in them. Yet the Lord requires us to have it richly dwelling in us. "Let the word of Christ dwell in you richly in all wisdom; teaching and admonishing one another in psalms and hymns and spiritual songs, singing with grace in your hearts to the Lord" (Colossians 3:16).

Throughout this book I have tried to quote as many scriptures as possible, where applicable to my text, as a guidance to you readers on the importance of the word. You cannot just be content with reading it once a week when you attend a church service of maybe three hours. I believe, based on the way our physical bodies need food daily, in the same way we need the word daily. If you eat three times a day, make an effort of reading the word of God three times also—and then if you fail to do so, know it's just the same way as if you missed a meal in a day. How do you feel? Then can you imagine how your spirit suffers every time you skip a spiritual meal, whether in word, prayer, psalms, and so forth? In politics, every Christian has his or her rightful position biblically of interceding for the leaders for the free course of the word of God to proceed in a peaceful way when leaders have been chosen out of prayers. Many Christians also become like other citizens, complaining of who they want and don't want. I often wonder whether God or men give authority to rule nations. "I exhort therefore, that first of all, supplications, prayers, intercessions and giving of thanks be made for all men; for kings and for all that are in authority, that we may lead a quiet and peaceable life in all godliness and honesty for this is good and acceptable in the sight of God our Savior" (1 Timothy 2:1–3).

God's word is systematic and orderly. When we pray for all men, we obey the Lord and not men. When we pray for leaders, we are still obeying God, not man, and we do ourselves a favor since we shall live peaceful lives. All those in authority are to be upheld in prayers if there is any harmony expected. I wonder how many Christians would prefer to be stepping on dead bodies as they try to preach the gospel to the living ones. When there isn't peace in a nation, there

## Fear Not; God Is in Charge

are wars that leave many dead. When we pray for leaders and all in authority, we also create freedom of worship and preach the gospel without hindrances. If we fail to pray for leaders, drunkards and all other malefactors will choose leaders blindly and most likely their own counterparts. What will happen? The word also clearly states that righteousness exalteth a nation, but sin is a reproach to a nation. If we expect good leadership, then we have to pray, even for those choosing leaders so they will be led by the Holy Spirit to choose the right candidates. Nothing is too hard for God. Only believe and take your rightful position, and God will bless you in a mighty way. On the other hand, obeying leaders makes us good citizen unlike the malefactors who are always breaking the laws of the nation. May God help us not to fear as we obey those in leadership, even if others aren't obeying them. Remember that you aren't supposed to follow a multitude to do evil. Obey individually, and you will receive your pay from the Lord Himself.

So we clearly see that if you expect any peace of your surroundings, be it at home, church, place of work, nation, and so forth, you must be interceding for the leaders respectively, praying on their behalf whether they are for you or against you. You obey the word of God, and you have peace. Reality will convict our mortal bodies not to pray for those who are against us, but the Bible tells us to pray for them. The spirit is always willing, but the flesh is always weak. In every situation, the word expects us to be grateful and joyous in the Lord. "Rejoice evermore, pray without ceasing. In everything give thanks for this is the will of God in Christ Jesus concerning you" (1 Thessalonians 5:16–18). *Everything* here means simply "all." The message is not in some things rejoice, but for others, especially the negative ones, please don't rejoice. The Bible never states this but simply says "in everything." One singer encouraged me as he sang that in all he would see, be it good or bad, for approval or not, he would always be looking upon the Lord so that God will give him rest when He comes. This singer must have had a personal battle, and as he battled within himself, I tend to think the Holy Spirit inspired and encouraged him with this song. It is good to be chewing cud when there is need. May God help us to have His word dwelling richly in us, which is the determining factor of good success in this universe. God Himself, after the death of His servant Moses, encouraged Joshua as he took over the leadership of the Israelites so that the word was all he needed to be successful.

"This book of the law shall not depart out of thy mouth: but thou shall meditate therein day and night, that thou mayest observe to do according to all that is written therein: for then thou shalt make thy way prosperous, and then thou shall have good success" (Joshua 1:8). From this text I get a special revelation on the words "good success." This means there is bad and good success. For sure if you are a thief and succeed in stealing, this is bad success; but if you succeed because of trusting the Lord to supply all your needs according to His riches in glory, then this is good success. Therefore, good success is what originates from the laws of the Lord and obedience thereof. Our way of life is a determining factor of fear because when Christians are fully surrendered to the living Christ, their lives are transformed and become like the Christians who became witnesses of the risen Lord and Savior. These types of Christians can never fear. why? They have had such a good relationship with the Lord that all they can afford to do is witness about Him without fretting. Knowing our position when we trust the Lord will help us not to entertain fear. Once we truly know we have entered a new life in Christ, we cannot afford to fear. We are confident that we are a new creation in Him.

We know that the battle isn't ours, but all we need to do is stand firm and see the victory of the Lord. Children fear many things; even a barking dog can scare a child to a great extent. In the same way, if we remain spiritual children who don't grow, we will be prone to fretting every now and then. God's will for all Christians is that we leave our childish things and be mature spiritually. "Brethren, be not children in understanding: howbeit in malice, be ye children: but in understanding be men" (1 Corinthians 14:20). Once we forsake spiritual childishness and become grown-ups, we can never fret anymore. How do we grow spiritually? The same way physical

## Fear Not; God Is in Charge

growth requires nourishment of every kind of food, so do we need the nourishment of our souls in prayers, word, fellowship, service to God, and so forth. It is when we grow up that we won't fear.

Nevertheless, there are times when even grown-ups fear; for example, if you are residing somewhere and bandits have been attacking neighbors several times, there is always some fear. Everybody gets so keen and equipped that to some extent he or she almost stays awake the whole night. When we fear spiritually, we should equip ourselves with every spiritual armor, even as the word says, "Finally, my brethren, be strong in the Lord, and in the power of his might. Put on the whole armor of God, that ye may be able to stand against the wiles of the devil" (Ephesians 6:10–11). Fears of spiritual grown-ups are attacks of the enemy, and we conquer them by equipping ourselves fully. We are being encouraged in this text that we should be strong—not in our own strength but in the Lord and His power. The armor we are expected to put on isn't earthly armor but the armor of God. With this, we cannot afford to fear. Grown-ups graduate from one step of glory to another, and we are also encouraged that we shall grow continually until in the end we shall be like Jesus. Steps of growth lead to the anointing of the Lord in our lives. When we are anointed of God, we cannot fret, and we do things not because others are doing them but because God has said so in His word. We serve God in our respective churches, not just because we are called on but because we are inspired in our spiritual maturity age.

Churches with grown-ups don't experience many hassles because every grown-up Christian will feel like he or she is sinning when he or she isn't serving God in one way or the other. A grown-up will tithe faithfully and regularly because God has taught him or her to do so in Malachi 3:10. "Bring ye all the tithes into the storehouse, that there may be meat in mine house and prove me now herewith, saith the Lord of hosts, if I will not open you the windows of heaven and pour you out a blessing that there shall not be room enough to receive it." This verse is clear to a mature Christian who will tithe to obey God and not to please his pastor. There is no business here between the pastor and this Christian. The business is between you

Christian and God. It says "saith the Lord," not "saith the pastor." Amen. The pastor may not know how much you have, but God, the giver and creator, knows.

If you earn so much money, the pastor may speculate that you are very faithful in tithing because of the good figure of your tithe, but before God, it might not be *all your tithe*. It is only a childish Christian who won't tithe all; otherwise, if it's not at all, then you are cornering God, and you will be in for it because the word is clear that God isn't mocked. A mature Christian will take his or her tithe to the storehouse. "What is a storehouse in this case?" you may ask as you read this phrase. Your storehouse is your home church, where you fellowship, and not where you visit or another ministry you are involved in. So many immature Christians have been trapped by their ignorance in this issue that you find a good Christian giving to a ministry that isn't his or her home church. What do I mean by a home church? It's a church where you regularly feed spiritually, where you take your problems or where you are counseled. If you lose one of your beloved, it's where you take the bad and good news that befalls you and expect others to carry your burden in all their capability. That is your home church.

You could be involved in other fellowship several times, in preaching, and so forth. Please be informed that these aren't home churches but mere fellowships for you when you are there. The way we have our normal homes is the same we should be having home churches. Unfortunately, some Christians are what I would call "nomadic" Christians, who move from one church to another. If you are such, it may be due to a lack of knowledge; identify yourself with one church and be a permanent member. Mature Christians will give preference to their home church responsibilities, not to other fellowships or churches where they visit and preach. By this, I mean you cannot be mature and leave a home church function without the permission of your pastor to be in another church's function. In my tribe, we have a saying: "*Ndungitiga nyumba yaku king'eu ugacokie murango kwene.*" This is to say, you cannot leave your house with the door wide open just to go and close another person's or neighbor's door. This would be very foolish indeed. In the same way, it would be spiritual foolishness to do what I have mentioned above. It is also a big sign of immaturity. You owe your home church pastor or elders respect, which you will be blessed for. Respect them who rule over you (Romans 13). When you tithe faithfully, you do yourself a favor before God and not before the pastor. Why do I say this? Because you are obeying the word of God, your giver and creator.

I have personally experienced God's blessing in tithing many times, but I want to share with every reader of this book one particular way I was so blessed that I also wondered about the faithfulness of God. In 1995, I attended the end-of-the-year overnight meeting in my home church. After midnight, I made a resolution in my heart and requested something from God. I even stood to be prayed for, though I didn't mention the need, but I lifted it to God. I needed a salary increment to a figure I specified to God. That was then, 1996. I promised to tithe faithfully as I had always done aforetime. At the end of January 1996, no salary increment came, but I reasoned with my God and purposed that with or without the increment, I would still tithe the figure I had specified to God during the overnight meeting. I took a step and requested my boss for the same, but he told me to wait, and I agreed. I continued tithing for eight months, yet there was no salary increase. I resolved to record daily miracles from God. For example, if it happened that I met a friend who paid fare or bought lunch for me, I counted that as a miracle. Believe it or not, by the end of every month, I always found out that I received the figure I had specified or more but never less. Amen. Our God is faithful!

We carry unnecessary burdens just because we don't take them to our Savior, who is always waiting to lift them from us. All we need to do is let Him know in prayer. I had told Jesus my need, and I was fully assured that it was recorded well in heaven, awaiting His approval but never forgotten. Through the many things I have gotten from God through prayers and by faith, I have learned and can confidently say that God has no dustbin for dumping our prayers. He always keeps them safely, awaiting the appointed time. Yes, He may delay according to our time, but He always intervenes at the right and appointed time, and no wonder the word came to prophet Habakkuk when he was almost giving up. "And the Lord answered me, and said, Write the vision, and make it plain upon tables, that he may run that readeth it, For the vision is yet for an appointed time, but at the end it shall speak, and not lie: though it tarry, wait for it; because it will surely come, it will not tarry" (Habakkuk 2:2–4).

From these words we see that patience is paramount for our heavenly journey, and as mentioned earlier, we need to be mature spiritually so we manage to bear even when the answers of our prayers seem to delay. Children are very impatient, and they like their needs met immediately unlike the grown-ups. Therefore, the more mature we are spiritually, the more we shall have patience over issues in our Christian lives. After some months I remember that my husband asked me about that figure since he knew my salary, and I told him what I had promised my God. I tell you spiritual things have to be individual as you obey God individually. and no wonder Peter and the other apostles said, "We had rather obey God rather than man" (Acts 5:29). My husband is a Christian, so he had no problem, but he just asked because he knew how much I was earning. But the decision was made between me and God, and I believe if all we do is for the glory of God, then He will give our counterparts the right comprehension of our decision without any confusion. Our God isn't of confusion but of order, even in family matters. All we need to be careful about is involving Him in all we do. Obedience to God's word is personal, but the blessings will be to all you relate to, such as parents, husbands, wives, children, friends, and so forth but never in a multitude.

At this juncture, I know someone will ask, "She is married yet tithes separately?" Yes, I do it separately because when you wed, I always hear the pastor say as he reads the word, "The two shall be one flesh." I have never heard or read that the two shall be one spirit. Amen. Your spouse may not feel convicted to make such a move like the one I took by faith. My husband is a Christian, and I don't undermine his spiritual stand, but what I mean is that you need to have a personal touch to see personally in the spiritual realm. When miracles happen, I go and share with him, and he praises the Lord, but the touch

## Fear Not; God Is in Charge

and conviction have to be personal. That year, 1996, I received the greatest miracle in my life. It was so big that to date I have never and will never forget it. I went abroad on a mission through the church to sing in Switzerland. Everything was cared for, and I never used a single coin, but God did it, even the passport expenses and follow-up. It was the church and others, including friends, my husband, the women's department of our church, and even my boss, whom God touched for what I needed for my travel. May God continue to bless all those God has touched in one way or the other.

Others were behind us in prayers and fasting as they pleaded to God to pour His anointing on us, and we saw the Lord move mightily as we ministered to the white people in singing for two weeks because nothing is too hard for God. I know those who normally board airplanes and go abroad for different missions and businesses to various countries may not see this as a miracle, but to me it was and will remain a big one. I had never even desired to travel just because I couldn't see that a way would ever come, but God almighty made it possible.

I regard this as part of that year's miracle and blessing for my tithing by faith. In this area of tithing, I have been so blessed that no one can stop me from sharing it with others who are reading this book. Take a step and start tithing if you haven't been doing so, and you will be surprised to see how much you have been losing as a result of not tithing. Once, God quickened me on tithing my time. In a day we have twenty-four hours, and 10 percent of this is two hours and forty minutes; within a day and a night you have two hours and forty minutes for God. I began tithing the same by reading the word, praying, singing or composing songs, writing articles on Christian living, attending fellowships, sharing His love with someone, attending women's meetings, attending church choir practice, and so forth. I tell you my life hasn't been the same. I find these hours too short, and most of the time, I don't even complete what I set myself to do for God within this time limit.

I have also noted that my relationship with God has improved tremendously. When we obey God in tithing, we experience a spiritual breakthrough, and you find yourself always eager to do the work of God. As I continued in this, I found myself releasing my all to God, and before then I never used to do that, and mind you I was still saved. God in return started opening doors for me to serve Him to make sure these times were spent on Him. To date, I find the work of God so much that I don't even afford to do even a big fraction. Mission invitations, one after another, come in different ways and to different places, either to sing or to preach. When I get this invitation, it may be to share in women's meeting in other churches. I have no choice but to read the word of God, pray, and seek the presence of God for the proper message for that particular group; I don't always know whatever they are going through. I also started seeing that God has a divine purpose for my serving Him. Initially, I had always speculated that my call was more for the youth than for other age-groups in the body of Christ. I got saved when I was in school, and I had always shared and interacted with the youth. Even after school, I continued to be in youth leadership in different churches up to the time I got married. I handed over my office of being a youth group secretary when I married. So with all these indicators, I always convinced myself that my call was to the youth.

Once, I was invited to a women's meeting in a different church to minister. I shared, and people were blessed. I was requested to return again. I went, and mind you, all these were in different churches, not my home church. People from different churches extended their invitation to their respective churches, and I did not hesitate to go unless there was a function at my home church where my participation was needed. Even as I mentioned earlier, we need to be mature with our respective home churches. God is mighty and not a respecter of any man.

As a singer when composing songs, I find myself, for reasons I also don't comprehend well, covering almost all age-groups in the songs, and this has helped me to be humble before God for His work at His own convenient time. I always have a prayer before God. "Lord, I am willing, I am availing myself for You, and I am yielding to Thee, oh Lord, for Thy use." This I felt persuaded to share because before I embarked on giving all to God—that is money, time, strength, and heart—I never used to be that way. When we surrender all to God, He will use us in a mighty way. Your spiritual eyes will be opened to see that there is much work, but the laborers are few; and in the process, you will surrender to be one of the laborers.

Today, if you surrender *all* and not just *some*, you will never be the same anymore, irrespective of your age, status, family background, and so forth. Even my going to church changed tremendously. I started praying before going that God would minister to me the way He saw necessary, that I would be a blessing also to the body of Christ in whichever way He would see fit in me, praying for the ministers of the gospel and all others, as recorded in 2 Timothy 2:1–2. This became part of me, and I started enjoying prayers. I urge you, dear reader, to start giving to God, and I believe that because of the way I was raised spiritually, you will also experience the same breakthrough, and God will bless you.

On the other hand, I would not like to be one sided and promise you bread and butter as you release yourself to the almighty God. No. One thing I have experienced to date is that when you purpose to surrender to God, you become a target to the devil, but glory be to God because the one in us is greater than the one in the world.

Since I surrendered to serve God, the enemy has been on the rampage, but I thank God that He is a faithful God who will never leave or forsake us. He always seeks an opportunity to attack my ministry for God through sicknesses of children, lack of house girls when I am about to go for a mission, misunderstandings in the office, and so forth. But all in all, I can confidently confess and say that I always get a quickening sign from the Holy Spirit and address the particular hindrance and also the devil openly. "Like it or not, Satan, I am going on that mission," I say, and I have always seen the victory of the Lord. In the service of God, you must be biblically violent if you are to succeed, and I am excited when I read, "And from the days of John the Baptist *until now*, the kingdom of heaven suffereth violence and the violent take it *by force*" (Matthew 11:12, emphasis added).

One day I had set to pray and fast for missions and the body of

Christ. I started having some stomach pains, which normally come when one is hungry. I felt tempted to cancel the fasting and pray only, but the Holy Spirit quickened me, and I knew it was the trick of the devil. I went to the toilet and forcefully argued with the devil. I reached a point and told God, "If I die because of fasting in these pains, I better die, but I won't taste any food." I wrestled for about twenty minutes in tears and through fists in the air because we fight principalities of the air. I tell you, by the time I finished my prayers, all the pains had disappeared completely, and I was as peaceful as a satisfied, sleeping baby. If it weren't for that spiritual violence, I could have eaten and argued that God would understand, but God is good because His word is true and alive forever more. Amen.

There is a lot of pleasure when we obey the word of God because He will be no man's debtor. Once you remind God of what His word says, I tell you all will be well, since He has to fulfill it. "Then said the Lord unto me, Thou hast well seen: for I will hasten my word to perform it" (Jeremiah 1:12). God is eagerly waiting for you to remind Him of His word, and He will hasten to perform it. If you give to God, you are reminding and obeying His word in Malachi, and He will definitely give you the desires of your heart. If you give Him your strength in service, He will bless you with long life and cover you with His glory.

I have also noted that the more you serve God, the younger you look than your years. There was a lady in our church whose services for God always challenged me a lot. She was a Sunday school teacher for a long time, a women's leader and an evangelist; and most of the times she was out on missions. On Sundays, she was always among the first people as a Sunday school teacher yet in her age.

Many relax as they reason that the younger generation can do the work, but praise be to God, who is impressed not by age or status but by availability, willingness, and yielding of available vessels. She was quite old, and I tell you, you would ponder the fact that she appeared to be in her early thirties, yet she was over fifty years. She had grandchildren, and when we walked together, frankly speaking you could think she was younger than me and I was by then in my

## Fear Not; God Is in Charge

early thirties. I went on missions with her, and she was always the one who woke us up for morning devotions and other meetings. God also likes honoring those who honor Him with all they have and more so in the service as they forsake all they have for His sake. In spiritual maturity, there is no fear, but attack of the fear can be there, and we can confidently say like David, "The Lord is my on my side; I will not won't fear: what can man do unto me?" (Psalm 119:6). Yes, fear may come as an attack, but we can be confident in our God, who is mighty. We are like trees planted by the river's side when we mature in the things of God. This tree differs from the other trees just because of where it is planted. When drought comes, it's not affected because there is a source of supply of all its nutrients unlike the others planted far from the river.

As Christians, we are like the other human beings on planet earth, but the major difference is that we are firmly grounded on a rock, which is a good foundation. This rock is Jesus. When storms of life come, like economy difficulties, hunger, and daily needs, we are in the same earth where inflation comes, but our hope isn't only in our daily income. It is more than that; the Ebenezer God is with us. Jehovah Jireh, who provides, is in control. Jehovah Rapha, our healing, is present to see all we are undergoing. Jehovah Sharma, our peace, is around to tell us, "Hold your peace" and so forth. This, our mighty God, is able to make rivers flow in the wilderness and to make ways in the thick forest. This knowledge of our God makes the difference in mature Christians.

As mentioned earlier, we fail in life because of failing to know our rights as the children of God. Failing to have the word of God dwelling richly in us makes us poor people both spiritually and physically. What I want to say here is this: The enemy will torment you with depression because you don't have the word dwelling richly in you. You start complaining to the extent of speculating you are bewitched. What does the word say? "Come unto me all ye that labor and are heavy laden, and I will give you rest" (Matthew 11:28).

God comprehends our every circumstance, be it good or bad, and He has laid down rules and regulations for us to follow, his word. As we hearken and follow Him faithfully, we will always find a word to hold onto at the hour of every need. A laboring person with different hassles is normally so disturbed that if there is no way to have the burden released from him or her, he or she can easily get depressed, and hence the Lord is calling such for the rest of their souls. Jesus has volunteered Himself to bear the burdens of our lives; and if we respond to His call, all will be cared for, and we find rest.

There are some people who prefer to stay with their burdens than to give them to the Lord, and for such, nobody can be blamed since Christ has offered all for our sake. There was a Maasai *moran* who went hunting in a game reserve. He spotted an antelope and was very happy. He was equipped for hunting, and so he drew near to the antelope. Nearby there was a lion at quite a distance that had ambushed the same antelope for meat, but this masai managed to spear the antelope first, and it fell dead to the ground. He was thrilled that he could now enjoy the meat soon after.

The lion ran to get the dead antelope, which the masai lifted and carried shoulder high, running with it. This masai was lucky since there happened to be a tourist in that same reserve in a Nissan vehicle. He saw the masai running, with the lion behind him, and he sympathized greatly. He pleaded with him to leave the antelope and enter the vehicle for safety, but the masai was so committed to the antelope that he couldn't drop it for the lion.

The lion now drew near him, and the tourist pleaded all the more, but the victim didn't heed his words. When the masai tried to enter the vehicle, the horns of the antelope wouldn't allow him to enter easily through the door; they were a hindrance. The tourist continued to plead with him to drop the animal and save his life, but stupendous enough, he chose to cling to the antelope for meat than to save his only life. This good tourist couldn't contend further, and since he sensed danger to himself, he drove off, leaving the masai. The lion came, furiously knocked the masai down to death, and ate the antelope. The masai foolishly lost the antelope and his life for greed of what was temporal.

## Fear Not; God Is in Charge

This true story is applicable in our spiritual way, which is also very clear. The comparison is indicated below for a good understanding:

Maasai *moran*—you as a person
Tourist—Jesus as the driver
Nissan—salvation
Antelope—sins which clings so close to us
Lion—the devil

The Bible clearly states that the devil roars like a lion, looking for someone to devour. As mentioned earlier, God is always calling us to reason out with Him for our sins, which He wishes to cleanse if we respond to His call. Like the foolish masai, we keep on clinging to temporal things, which lead us to eternal damnation.

Christ is always pleading with us, "Come unto me all ye that labor," yet we proceed, giving out reasons like this foolish Maasai, who loved meat more than his own life. Christ is calling us for salvation, and He will be the professional driver in control of our heavenly journey, yet you continue to give reasons and questions, such as, What if I backslide? What about my girlfriend? What about that business and the corruption involved? What about my job (and I need money)?

My friend, I tell you if that Maasai had known he would lose both the antelope and his life, he would have hearkened to the pleas of that good tourist. You are also holding on to very temporal things, which you will end up losing and miss heaven also. If I were you, I would choose life and forsake all others, who seem very appealing but for a time, and their end is an endless sorrow. Whatever you are holding on to, know that if it's not the Lord Jesus, be well informed that it is like broken cisterns that cannot hold water. Come to Jesus if you don't want to perish after this life. All you have entangling yourself in is coming to an end, and you will be no more.

## Chapter 7

# Fear Not if You Trust the Lord

MY ANSWER TO this whole chapter is a big no. So long as we know that nothing is too hard for God, we can in no way fear or entertain fretting in our lives. When we are confident that the Lord is able to meet all our needs, whatever they may be, we can be as peaceful as a small baby, resting in the mother's arms and waiting to suckle the already-waiting breast with the already-sufficient milk. The only sign the baby gives to the mother is crying, which is symbolic to lifting our voices to God in prayer. A singer said, "Oh what needless pain we bear, all because we do not carry everything to God in prayer." I quite agree with this singer because, if you fail to pray, then you have to fret whenever disaster strikes. Why? Because you haven't taken everything you would undergo to God in prayer. So I would likewise say that a Christian may choose to fear by disobeying God's word, which is a light to our feet.

When we obey, we will pray because the word tells us plainly, "Pray without ceasing" (1 Thessalonians 5:17). It's very hard to enter a temptation of fearing when you are praying. The more you pray, the more confident you become in the Lord. Fast because Christ whom we imitate also fasted. In the strength of our physical food alone, it's hard to overcome some difficulties. Therefore, we should

## Fear Not; God Is in Charge

regularly learn to oppress our physical bodies as we skip our meals for prayers to uplift the spiritual part in our lives. Personally, I have experienced that when I am too full, the feeling is normally very hard, and even it's a bother since my body likes to relax in a siesta. Praying sometimes is very hard work as you wrestle with the principalities of the air, since our battle isn't physical. "For though we walk in the flesh, we do not war after the flesh; for the weapons of our warfare are not carnal but mighty through God to the pulling down of strongholds; casting down imaginations and every high thing that exalteth itself against the knowledge of God and bringing into captivity every thought to the obedience of Christ" (2 Corinthians 10:3–5).

These scriptures are self-explanatory of a real spiritual battle that needs one who has denied himself or herself some pleasures of this world, like even meals. As mentioned, I have many times experienced that prayers, when you have to really struggle with the forces of the enemy in the air, are very effective, and they always avail much more than just mere prayers, which you pray when relaxed. In an earlier chapter, I shared prayers that cost you something, and they are exactly the same thing I am also endeavoring to expound on further. It's when you are napping that a particular strange message will make you fret; otherwise, if you are busy in one way or the other in the Lord, all will be received in awareness as you put to practice whatever you could be reading in the Bible, praying, sharing with another believer, and so forth to that strange event. Rejoice for whatever causes any alarm in our day-to-day life because the word tell us plainly, "Rejoice in the Lord always and again I say rejoice," and our faith is also built up. When we walk in the light of God in His word, all our impossibilities will be regarded as God's opportunities in our lives. We have many examples in the Bible of such opportunities that seemed like impossibilities to man first.

When the Israelities were in captivity, God allowed this to happen so they could see and witness His greatness over Pharaoh. The word clearly says that God hardened Pharaoh's heart several times. Why?

He wanted them to know that all impossibilities are possibilities with Him and for their own good as His called ones.

> And I will harden Pharaoh's heart, that he shall follow after them; and I will be honored upon Pharaoh and upon all his host; that the Egyptians may know that I am the Lord. And they did so. (Exodus 14:4)

> And the Lord hardened the heart of Pharaoh king of Egypt and he pursued after the children of Israel and the children of Israel went out with an high hand. (Exodus 14:8)

When God hardened the heart of Pharaoh, the situation became an impossibility to the Israelites, although He had promised them deliverance through Moses. As a result, they started complaining. "And the children of Israel cried out unto the Lord, and they said unto Moses, because there were no graves in Egypt, hast thou taken us away to die in the wilderness? wherefore hast thou dealt thus with us, to carry us forth out of Egypt" (Exodus 14:10). They didn't see the impossibility as an opportunity God wanted to use to build their faith in Him. Oh, if they had known what deliverance was ahead of them, they would have rejoiced in the Lord for everything.

In this situation every Israelite knew God isn't a man that He should lie or a son of man to repent of His promises. The Red Sea was before them, and looking behind, the chariot of Pharaoh was after them when God hardened his heart. They saw only with their naked eyes, and they began to complain against their leader, Moses. As a leader, he looked up from where his help came from. The Lord talked to him like to a friend, and he obtained another power and was able to confidently tell the Israelites, "Fear ye not, stand still, and see the salvation of the Lord which he will show to you today: for the Egyptians whom ye have seen today, ye shall see them again no more forever. I the Lord shall fight for you, and ye shall hold your peace" (Exodus 14:13–14).

It was the Lord through Moses who encouraged them with a "Fear not," which was sufficient for them that day but seemed so hard to them. It is when we have a word from God to hold on to that we can overcome the daily fretting that comes to us. Therefore, with the right word for a particular situation, we cannot fear. Yes, the Israelites feared and complained because they did not have a word from God. Immediately they were given the word by Moses from God, they stopped fearing and stood still. So they also had to take an action of "standing still," and they saw the salvation of the Lord. When we get the word as we pray, read the Bible, learn from fellowships, hear from a song, and so forth, we need to hold on to that word and stand still as we wait for God to do the rest for us. Our role is just to obey what the word says, and He will accomplish the rest for us. Here I would like to say that some Christians behave like children, wanting things to happen their way and at their own set time. But God's ways aren't our ways; neither are His plans like ours. Glory be to His holy name because His plans and ways are always the best for us. God is never late or too early, but He comes and intervenes at the right time. God's right time may be late to you and even so late that you felt like giving up, but it's always the best and sure time without any regrets.

From the above case of the Israelites, I believe they would have expected God to intervene before Pharaoh's chariots followed them, but we see that God allowed it so they could see His mighty deliverance. In the same way in our lives, God may allow you to go through a very hard situation deliberately so you can see His mighty intervention. The greater the hassle, the greater and more thrilling are the miracles and deliverance of the Lord.

# Lazarus's Sickness and Death (John 11:1–44)

This was a similar situation when Lazarus died. Jesus had been informed in good time, but He deliberately delayed for two days, and Lazarus died. When Martha saw Jesus from far, she commented, "If thou hast been here, my brother could not have died" (v. 20). We see that Jesus knew what was to happen when He said, "This sickness is not unto death, but for the glory of God, that the Son of God might be glorified thereby" (v. 4).

It was with this knowledge that all things were working out for God's glory. Jesus decided to delay for two good days where He was, but later He told His disciples to accompany Him into Judea (v. 7). Always those who accompany us in this journey may not encourage us to press on by faith, but they will in many ways discourage us as they speculate that they are assisting us. In this episode, this happened because His disciples told him, "Master, the Jews of late sought to stone thee; and goes thou thither again?" (v. 8). This was a discouragement to His mission, but the disciples were saying it in good faith for security purposes. They feared that He might be harmed. Jesus knew His call and mission well, so He proceeded. We need to know our call such that even when the so-called good advice comes to us, we still press on toward our mission for God. It's when you surely know your call that hindrances of all kinds and through anyone won't stop you from doing what God has commissioned you to do. We can never stop advice from the people around us as we serve God, but we can stop any hindrances for our mission if we know our call well. We can be confident to say all in all, "The Lord has commissioned me, and I have answered His call that wherever He sends me, I will go; and whatever He wants me to do, I will obey." Remember, if you aren't doing the greatest commission, you are obviously doing the greatest omission. It is trusting and obeying God that will bring success in this world.

Once, God laid a burden on me to go for a mission with a certain group in my church. I had always gone for missions when I was single,

## Fear Not; God Is in Charge

but this time, it was the first conviction after marriage. I had my second-born kid, who was only one year and five months old and was breast feeding. I really sought God about the trip in prayers and fasting. and God gave me words to hold on to.

Exodus 33, the whole chapter, was encouraging, but in particular was the following: "And I will send an angel before thee and I will drive out the Canine, the Ammonite, and the Hittite and the Parasite, the Hivite and the Jebusite" (v. 2). This taught me so much and encouraged me that as I prepared, God would send an angel before me to drive out every hindering powers and circumstances.

"I know thee by name, and thou hast also found grace in my sight" (v. 12). This was a confirmation that despite my having a small breast-feeding kid, God knew and comprehended well, and I had found grace in His sight to be used in that mission.

"Now therefore, I pray thee, if I have found grace in thy sight, show me now thy way, that I may know thee, that I may find grace in thy sight: and consider that this nation is thy people. And he said, *My presence shall go with thee, and I will give thee rest.* And he said unto him, *If thy presence go not with me, carry us not up hence*" (vv. 13–15, emphasis added). These scriptures had a deep meaning up to now because I continued to reason with God, and He continued to press me all the more until I surrendered in repentance. "My presence shall go with thee and I will give thee rest" (v. 14). This was a repeated confirmation as we note his angel's presence in verse 2. Based on verse 15, I said to God, "If thy presence won't go with me, Lord, I won't go for that mission." The confirmation I needed here mostly was because of the kid's health. Many mothers understand that a small kid needs to be warm enough to prevent cold, flu, and other cold-related ailments. Even in the monthly baby clinics, we are admonished to keep the babies warm without much exposure to cold weather.

Other words God continued to press on me included John 12:3–8. "Then took Mary a pound of ointment of spikenard, very costly, and anointed the feet of Jesus, and wiped his feet with her hair: and the house was filled with the odor of the ointment. Then saith one of his disciples, Judas Iscariot, one which should betray him, why was not this ointment sold for three hundred pence, and given to the poor? This he said, not that he cared for the poor; but because he was a thief, and had the bag, and bare what was put therein. Then said Jesus, Let her alone: against the day of my burying hath she kept this. For the poor always ye have with you; but me ye have not always." Through verse 3, God revealed to me that my availability was like the ointment Mary had, which was costly, but she chose to anoint the feet of Jesus with the same. As much as my kid was small, the Lord needed my participation in that mission. Based on verses 7–8, all my reasoning within me was completed under these scriptures because I had always had more time before and after, but this mission was just for a particular period. With all these challenges, exaltations, and convictions, I surrendered and decided I was to go, and hence I forwarded my name among the list of the other attendants.

The biggest hassle now came within me; would my husband allow me? Would he understand? All these questions hovered within me, and every time I prepared to ask my husband for permission, I found myself confounded to break the news. I could pray during the day and decide to tell him in the evening; then I could hesitate, and days continued passing. One night before we slept, I told him but still stammered. First, I shared all the words God had given me, and then I started with, "I have a burden in me and whatever you will see me doing, please comprehend it's because of the burden God is laying on me for His work." He didn't say anything for some time, and I stopped there.

After some time, he asked me, "What were you saying?"

I took a breath and said, "I'm feeling persuaded to go for this year's Easter mission."

His answer was such an exciting one. "If God has said and convinced you, what do you expect me to say? Amen." He didn't ask me about the kid since it was obvious I couldn't leave her since she was breastfeeding. I started thanking God as I prepared for the

## Fear Not; God Is in Charge

mission, this time confidently, since all round the almighty God had cleared the hindrances.

The devil was well informed of my advance preparations, but I encouraged myself since he always uses opposing powers through reasonable circumstances to hinder our service for our almighty God.

One day all the missioners were in a prayer meeting, as is normally done in our church, and we were summoned in front by the pastor, elders, and the entire church to pray for us as a team. After the meeting, one elder came and greeted me, and in a very concerned way, as the disciples did to Jesus, he asked me, "You are also going?"

I answered him confidently. "Yes."

"And the small one?"

I consequently and boldly answered all his questions without hesitation and with another big yes. He wondered and commented, "It's not fair with that little one. Can't you leave her?" I told him she was still breastfeeding. He left me, and I really understood the very good concern he had. As a father with his own kid, he knew what it means to leave or go with a kid for missions. This is one of the hindrances the foe brings when the Lord wants us out for His use. It's never easy and will never be easy, but we should violently fight those forces if the Lord thoroughly convicts us to serve Him. I said *thoroughly* because some people serve God for the sake of prestige. This cannot work in very sensitive circumstances; neither can there be blessings if it's not through conviction if a challenge comes. I didn't mistake our elder; neither did I feel guilty about going with the child because God had convicted me, and I had no doubt.

The night prior to the mission day (it was a Thursday night), my daughter started having an irritating cough. She vomited, but thank God her father was deeply asleep. I didn't want him to know because he could have revoked the permission because of the kid's health. Why did I do this? I realized the devil was against the whole thing and hence started to attack. Silently I pleaded to God in prayer and reminded Him of the words He had given me before this time, and she was well by the time the day broke. We need to keep on fighting fear, which the enemy uses through any available channel.

When we went for that mission, I saw the hand of God in a very special way, and every evening we were always in revival meetings in the church that had hosted us. The weather wasn't very comfortable for a kid, especially at night, but I never missed a single meeting. My kid came back without a slight cold or any complications, and I glorify God up to now for that. This taught me a lot that God is our shepherd. As a shepherd takes the flock out to feed, he equips himself with every armory necessary for his own flock against any beast. Yes, God wanted me to take Him as a real shepherd, who would look after my kid and myself.

What a wonderful shepherd we have in our almighty God. There are no regrets when we serve God, though the devil always tries to cheat us and persuade us that we will lose when we leave all for the sake of our maker. He is a liar and the father of all lies. Never trust or listen to him. Ignore him and serve your maker without fear. He will always oppose any step you take that will cause you to be more effective for God, but we should also and always resist his plans because he is a defeated fellow who never accepts defeat.

A few months later, I coincidentally met one of the women leaders in that church in town, and she told me that women had been so challenged to see a breastfeeding mother going out for missions. Their women's meetings and attendance had been revived, and I gave God all the glory and honor.

When we trust the Lord, we shouldn't fret but be courageous since we know Satan is always out to do everything possible to keep us from living for our able God. In the past, you may not have been attacked viciously by him, but the moment you embark, being on the move for God and taking steps in your faith, he rages and sets out for your downfall. Nevertheless, we are more than conquerors in Christ Jesus, and ours is just to hold on peacefully and let God fight the battle for us without wavering.

I am grateful to God that He protected us all as a family even when my kids were very young. She is normally inspired in the things

## Fear Not; God Is in Charge

of God at her age. Believe it or not, she is so much used by God even to challenge us as parents, but what I haven't understood to date is whether she knows when she is being used. For example, if you forget to pray for food, she quickly comments, "Oh, we did not pray for the food!" If she has food in her mouth, she puts it down. When you tell her to pray, she prays for forgiveness for failing to pray first. Other times she sings songs that are always applicable to the present situation at a particular time in the house. What I mean is, at times I go home so discouraged for one reason or another, but when I enter the house and greet everybody, she starts some stories and asks questions of different family members. Then she starts a song or chorus like:

Nitamwimbia Bwana, Kwa Kuwa yeye ameniona.
(I will sing unto the Lord for He has seen me in all undergoing.)

As earlier mentioned, I am a singer, and my kids used to join singing one of the songs in my album:

Ndingihota itari nawe Jesu.
(I cannot do anything without You, Jesus.)

Being spiritually alert and sensitive to the Holy Spirit, I always realized that God was ministering to me through this sweet daughter of mine. It's my prayer that she will grow from one step of glory to another, even as she grows physically. At times, when we are all seated in the sitting room, she can start a topic that will challenge us spiritually; this helped me a lot to grow in the things of God through her because He isn't a respecter of persons or personality. This encouraged me so much as a parent that we should always avail our children for God's blessings, anointing, and presence in Sunday schools, churches, crusades, and so forth. This is very biblical because we read in Genesis 48:8–16,

> And Israel beheld Joseph's sons, whom God hath given me in this place, and he said, Bring them, I pray thee

unto me and I will bless them. Now the eyes of Israel were dim for age, so that he could not see. And he brought them near unto him; and he kissed them, and embraced them. And Israel said unto Joseph, I had not thought to see thy face, and lo, God hath shewed me also thy seed. And Joseph brought them out from between his knees, and he bowed himself with his face to the earth. And Joseph took them both, Ephraim in his right hand toward Israel's left hand, and Manasseh in his left hand, towards Israel's right hand, and brought then near unto him. And Israel stretched out his right hand, and laid it upon Ephraim's head, who was the younger, and his left hand upon Manasseh's head, guiding his hands wittingly; for Manasseh was the firstborn. And he blessed Joseph, and said, God, before whom my father's Abraham and Isaac did walk, the God which fed me all my life long unto this day, the angel which redeemed me from all evil, bless the lads; and let my name be named on them and the name of my father's Abraham and Isaac; and let them grow into a multitude in the midst of the earth.

This scripture narrates how Joseph took his sons, Ephraim and Manasseh, to his father, Israel, to be blessed. He didn't just go alone, reasoning the way many reason these days that God would understand. No, he went with them, and Israel touched their heads as he spoke blessings on each of them. We need to take our children in the house of God and also in the service of God practically. At times, God's servants need to touch them physically as they pray for them and not just pray on their behalf. Amen. Their grandfather, Israel, spoke many blessings on these two lads (v. 16). Many times parents deny their children blessings from God and also their understanding of our service for God just because we don't put initiative and take them to the house of God, where we are serving.

God can use even our little ones to reach grown-ups because He

## Fear Not; God Is in Charge

isn't a respecter of persons; neither does He regard personalities. May God help us not to be ignorant when He speaks to us, using those people we least expect Him to use. My son was always very social from a tender age and it so happened that he was very free with his teacher. I believe God wanted to start preparing him for evangelism through this character at his early age. He was in first grade, second semester. I don't know how he began it, but he asked his teacher, "*Wewe umeokoka?*" (Are you saved?). I don't comprehend what she thought because she disciplined him. He never told me when he came home, but he told the father, who told me. I endeavored to befriend him to tell me what exactly had transpired between him and the teacher, and he repeated the same words he had told my husband. His father warned me that such discussions and freedom I had with my son of even sending him to greet the teacher wasn't good since it might affect his performance in school because of assumptions. I didn't want to prolong that issue. That teacher later continued to send my son to greet me, and one time my son told her that I sing and that I even sell gospel music CDs. She sent him to tell me to give her one so she could listen to it. At this juncture, I wanted to know how serious she was and also whether that freedom was self-imposed. I wrote a note, which I gave my son, requesting her to direct me to her home. I also asked him to say that when she was free, we could pay her a visit with my son and also take her the compact disc personally.

She replied to my note and explained nicely how to get to her place. So I confirmed the freedom was there and true. I still have that note with me, which is nicely and safely stored. I will never forget September 9, 1997. We had just finished praying for supper when my son told me, "Mum, my teacher said you should pray for her. She got saved." What a mighty God we serve, who isn't a respecter of persons. I believe with all my heart that the question my son passed to his teacher previously must have been a spiritual impact. God continued to use it to reach this teacher for His glory. The following day, she asked my son whether I had prayed for her, and he frankly told her, "She did not pray for you because she slept." This he also told me when he came home from school. It was such a shame to me to have been given a good spiritual task by that available vessel for God (my son), which I didn't fulfill. I was so much challenged that the following morning before he left for school, I requested that we hold hands and pray for his teacher. We prayed together, and I believe God honored our prayers. God challenged me through my son to intercede for his teacher. Praying is biblical, but since I had neglected it, He used my son to wake me up spiritually and do what He wanted me to do.

It's when we go with our children to the house of God that we shall build character in them of being eager to serve God as they watch us being busy for God in our respective churches. They will also have a desire to partake of the Lord's Table. We make it a habit of being with them when we partake ourselves. This I experienced many times with my kids when they were small that the Lord's Table is for saved people. He really fixed me one day in connection with that explanation. We consented to leave them at home, and we went to church with my husband because the weather was a bit chilly. He commented, "Mum, you don't want us to go to church and get saved so that we are also given that Lord's Table?" Well, he wanted to challenge me so that I could agree to go with them, but later I learned something from that comment on my own—that faith comes by hearing the word of God. We need to be where the word is taught to build our faith in the Lord, even to an extent of receiving the Lord into our hearts as a Savior. Let us learn to take our children where the word of God is, and when they grow up, they will have a desire for the same growing in them gradually.

It's funny the way we expect our youth to be in church when we didn't teach them to be in Sunday school when they were small. In my mother tongue, we have a saying: "*Muti urungagwo riria wi munyinyi*" (You can easily shape up a tree when it's small). It's ridiculous how we speculate that our youth can easily be changed by attending services and youth meetings, yet we leave them at home, watching murder films or playing rock music, as we reason out that they are too small to be taken to the house of our heavenly father. Of late I have had a revelation, and I have watched keenly and realistically; and I have found that most churches don't have young people. Why not? Because they are always where they think the action is (disco halls, cinema halls, sports grounds, and so forth). They weren't taught that there is any meaningful action in the churches since they were small, yet there is a lot of good, inspiring, and everlasting action in the churches. May God help us. This problem has resulted in a lack of respect by the youth to the old. Like in the time of Eli, we realize that most people are dying in the flowering age. There are no blessings from God since we have forsaken His ways. Parents, we are the root cause of all these problems. Let's return to God, who is always faithful to hear our cry of repentance. Another time I was wondering whether in ten years we shall have any old people based on the way things are.

> Wherefore the sin of the young men was very great before the Lord. (1 Samuel 2:17)

> Behold, the days come, that I will cut off thine arm, and the arm of thy father's house, that there shall not be an old man in thine house. And thou shalt see an enemy in my habitation, in all the wealth which God shall give Israel: and there shall not be old man in thine house for ever. And the man of thine, whom I shall not cut off from mine altar shall be to consume thine eyes, and to grieve thine heart and all the increase of thine house shall die in the flower of their age. And this shall be a sign unto thee, that shall come upon thy two sons, on Hopni and Phinehas, in one day they shall die both of them. (vv. 32–34)

If you read the whole second chapter of 1 Samuel, you comprehend well the brutal behavior of these sons of Eli, a priest in God's house.

They knew not the Lord nor regarded Him. We should desire to see our children knowing the Lord personally since our commitment to God cannot be transferred to them whatsoever. I don't believe God is unrighteous to forget our good works, and so if we continually let our children accompany us as we go to church and serve God, the Spirit of God will intervene in one way or another, and His fear will be in our children. If they misbehave once or twice when we are with them, we get a good chance of disciplining them when we are back home, and with this repeatedly together with prayers, God will be merciful to hear us.

One day I went to a wedding with my kids, and when the cake was being served, my son skipped the line and reached for the cake himself, and I was really embarrassed by his shameful act. Kids generally have bad habits unless they are disciplined, even as the Bible encourages every parent. "My son, keep thy father's commandments and forsake not the law of thy mother" (Proverbs 6:20). This verse clearly shows that both parents are needed in children's discipline. Both mother and father have a vital responsibility from God for each child. It is unfortunate that parents are slowly neglecting their roles as they push their kids to teachers and the world at large to teach them, but these are but mad masters without the parents, whom God saw fit to be the first discipliners in homes. All others will build on only the foundational character parents have prepared.

When we reached home, I made my son recall what he had done and told him it was bad, and he requested to be forgiven while crying. I couldn't just forgive him without a rod, so I slapped him and cautioned him not to repeat such a thing.

> Chasten thy son while there is hope, and let not thy should spare for his crying. (Proverb 19:18)

> Train up a child in the way he should go: and when he is old, he will not depart from it. (Proverb 22:6)

## Fear Not; God Is in Charge

These two verses give us courage for not sparing the rod. God has given us the responsibility of raising godly children, and in the end, we shall give an account. Back to my point, if I hadn't gone with my kids to the wedding, I wouldn't have witnessed that bad behavior of my son that needed to be worked on while there was still hope. If we leave them to house help, it becomes hard to know when they mess up since a mother and father are God appointed for the upbringing of children. I thank God that my son misbehaved in my presence because I wouldn't have believed it if somebody had reported the behavior to me. Maybe I would have argued that since I usually baked cakes for them time and again, such a thing couldn't have happened. Children will always be children and are bound to misbehave sometimes. But I believe it happened so I would know that nobody is ever so righteous as not to commit a sin. The devil is at work twenty-four hours a day, and hence he can even attack children, leading them to misbehave.

As we are busy for the Lord in our local churches, we should be keen enough to know that our first commitment to God is in our respective homes, which are regarded as Jerusalem in the Bible. "But ye shall receive power, after that the Holy Ghost is come upon you: and ye shall be witnesses unto me both in Jerusalem, and in all Judea, and in Samaria and unto the uttermost part of the earth" (Acts 1:8). I thank God for His systematic word, which when obeyed will always bring peace and joy in our lives. Though God commands us to go out in the power of the Holy Spirit, we are admonished to first start in Jerusalem (our homes), neighboring areas, and then other places. Many people obey this commandment of commission but start in Samaria. To me, it makes no sense to preach the word abroad or to other areas outside our houses and home areas when there is chaos right in Jerusalem. God had known this and hence admonished me on being systematic. I regard starting abroad with the gospel as a ladder; you can never start climbing from the top, but you have to climb from the bottom up, and systematically when you climb one stair, you go to the next one until you reach the expected place. It's also very ridiculous if you would have to climb a second or third stair, leaving the first one. This can make you fall easily, but you can successfully climb as you start with the first and then the second and so on. From the verse I have quoted, suppose you start in Judea, which is the second place recorded. What would become of Jerusalem? Yet you have to return there as your home. You may be so anointed and blessed as you see the hand of God at work in Judea, but if your Jerusalem has a problem, all the anointing and joy of serving God will be eroded immediately after you reach Jerusalem. Let me explain further for a better comprehension.

Suppose you leave your wife angry due to some disagreement in the morning over a domestic issue, but then you go to preach somewhere. It may be in a crusade. People will be blessed; maybe even the sick will be healed, but believe it or not, the moment you reach home, the wife will most likely be angrier than when you left her. Why? The devil who roars like a lion worked on her all day long and pressured her with such anger that can burst at your sight. These instructions could have been biblically applied in a systematic way if you could have followed them correctly. Jerusalem, Judea, Samaria—how do we reach them? Since temptations are sure to come in the form of disagreements, sickness, and so forth, we should be as wise as serpents and harmless as doves. Disagreements in families aren't unheard of, and our ways of handling them determine our peace, harmony, and victory over the enemy. To me, sorting out with the wife first and apologizing would have worked nicely and biblically. This way the devil wouldn't get an opportunity to use the wife because he isn't a respecter of personalities. Judean fruits can yield nicely and abide forever when Jerusalem is well cared for in its rightful priority. All this is obeying God because the Bible is clear and plain, even as the apostle Paul told the Romans, "Through mighty signs and wonders by the power of the Spirit of God, so that from Jerusalem and round about unto Illyricum, I have fully preached the gospel of Christ" (Romans 15:19). Here we see Jerusalem being given its rightful priority. In conclusion, all the Bible says about

## Fear Not; God Is in Charge

fear inspires us to overcome it by obeying God's word, and we can just overcome it—not on our own but only when we obey God's word. "Be of good courage, and He shall strengthen your heart all you that hope in the Lord" (Psalm 31:24).

## Chapter 8

# Why Some People Fear and Others Don't

THE REASON SOME people fear and other don't depends on each individual's trust and the position one has given God in his or her respective life. Throughout the year God encourages us not to fear because He is our God, Redeemer, refuge, hiding place, and strong tower; and the words He uses for encouraging us in the Bible are many. When we are in Christ, our God-given precious gift, we cannot fret. God always tells us, "Fear not." What are the reasons?

### He Is with Us

"God is our refuge and strength, a very present help in trouble" (Psalm 46:1–2). Trouble in the universe is the root course of fretting, and in this psalm, we see that trouble is already taken care of since God is a present help when trouble comes. As mentioned earlier, if you don't have the word of God dwelling richly in you, then it's obvious that you can fear. Why? You don't know what the word says about fear. The decision entirely depends on you—whether to fear by keeping the word of God in your heart richly or making it scarce and strange in your life. When we stay in the word of God—doing it or

## Fear Not; God Is in Charge

believing it—then we will fight every worry very easily. You should have a time to read the word of God if at all; you must overcome fear because it is the word in you that God quickens through the Holy Spirit to work though you at the very point of your specific need. Staying in the word gives us the confidence we need to fight fear in this heavenly race. The same word sets us free from all kinds of fears. Therefore, we should treasure the word, which can be used in a time of need.

We receive salvation freely through the grace of God, but to have the word, we need to make an effort to read and meditate on it. The Holy Spirit doesn't teach us the word, but He reminds us of what we have learned. Like computers, input determines output. So are our minds, as the Holy Spirit helps us remember what we have learned. Unless it's fed with information, you can retrieve nothing from its memory, yet it's very useful when it is properly fed with various information. Even after many years, you can easily get the information you fed into its memory when needed.

Our minds, when fed with the word of God, repeatedly act like a computer, and the operator is the Holy Spirit, who switches on the reminding button. Then we are able to overcome a certain hassle in life with that particular word, which you read a long time ago. Jesus overcame the devil with the word of God, and He was the Son of God. So we need to read the same word if we expect to have any success in overcoming fear.

Read Luke 4 carefully. After Jesus fasted forty days and forty nights, the devil shamelessly posed before Him a big temptation of food. Why? He knew Jesus was obviously hungry. The response of Jesus is reason and challenge enough to us today to store the word of God in our hearts and minds. The way Jesus replied to the devil clearly shows He had the word ready in his mind, not just checking it in a written form. The Spirit of God switched on the retrieving button, and the word was there for the devil's trap. We need to store the word in our hearts because the devil is always alert to our day-to-day living and the needs we have; and he always looks for an opportunity to get in the way when he knows we are in the presence of almighty God. He can use a certain need as an obstacle to our trusting God. Why didn't Jesus tell the devil who He was, the Son of God? I believe Jesus knew very well that the devil was no respecter of personalities or positions. He knew the only way to conquer him was with the word. Even today, the devil has never changed. He will never be a respecter of any person or their positions or titles. This is why we need the word whether we are reverends or bosses, or whether we're rich, poor, or educated enough to attain titles of being doctors, lecturers, philosophers, and so forth. God's degree of attaining victory over the enemy is His holy word. With the word richly dwelling in our lives, we can succeed in many things.

In these last days, the devil works tirelessly to bring down every zealous servant of God by denying him or her time to read the word because he knows it's the only sword for a Christian that defeats him. He has designed another fashion called "experience" in the work of God, but it's immaterial before God. God works daily to anoint available and yielded vessels, and this is not based on experience or long service. Goliath was experienced in battle, while David was not, yet David conquered him just by the word of the living God. "And the Philistine said to David, come to me, and I will give thy flesh unto the fowls of the air and to the beasts of the field. Then said David to the Philistine, Thou comest to me with a sword and with a spear and with a shield; but I come to thee in the name of the Lord of hosts the God of the armies of Israel whom thou hast defied" (1 Samuel 17:44–45).

Goliath boasted of his previous experience and counted on the same to defeat David, but David's strength was in the Lord; it was not his own. Here we see that David exalted God, even before approaching this Goliath with words; and hence, he was able to fight him victoriously. It is when we leave all to God to fight for us through His word that we shall attain the victory we need, and all glory will be to His holy name and not to ours. It is when we remove *our* and put *God* that all will be well in our lives. *Our* always brings pride, but *God* brings our total dependence on Him. David's trust was in God, so he couldn't fear the size of Goliath, his foe. The many problems we see, like big mountains in our lives, are like Goliath, and we are like

## Fear Not; God Is in Charge

David. We should see beyond them when we trust God. Many times we are scared by their size, and we even confess defeat, even before we involve God the way David did, yet there are three ways to overcome those mountains in our lives:

First, God may want you to go around the mountain to the other side. That is victory, and He will always give you enough grace and strength to walk all round it. Patience will be needed and depends entirely on the word as a light and lamp to your feet. As you go that long distance, before you reach your destination, there will be much discouragement through close kinsmen and allies, but God is faithful to encourage you throughout. Many will mock you the same way David's brothers mocked him, but he never gave up. He pressed on. The worst thing a Christian soldier can do is give up because of discouragement. We haven't been promised bread and butter, but it's war we need to fight courageously and win, and it will be regarded as "a good fight of faith."

When we take a step of faith as we go around the mountains, many of our brothers will blast us, but we should ignore them and continue with the Lord, who has called us. Elias, David's eldest brother, did the same to David, but David wasn't bothered. He pressed on, minding his own business with the Lord. "Elias's anger was kindled against David and he said, why comest thou down thither? and with whom hast thou left those few sheep in the wilderness? I know thy pride, and the naughtiness of thine heart; for thou art come down that thou mightiest see the battle. And David said, what have I now done? Is there not a cause? (1 Samuel 17:28–29). Even today, things haven't changed, and as we proceed to go around our mountains with the Lord, many will mistake us and think we are proud, blasting us openly. We should continue, and when we are through, the very same people who were initially against us will turn out to be our best allies as they commend us and glorify God. We will be acting in faith, and they will be acting on sight. Sight will be seen only after faith has yielded its rightful fruits. Many will be offended by our faith, or they will regard us as fools, but God always uses the foolish to challenge the wise of this universe. It's better to be a fool in the world and be wise in the things of God, even by obeying His words.

Elias was more concerned about the few sheep David had left unattended in the wilderness. There are still a few sheep some are worrying about instead of obeying God (for example, education, children, wives, husbands, jobs and so forth). This situation binds people so much that their attention is on only the sheep, and they can never leave them to go and serve their creator, worshipping the creation instead of the creator. May God help us to put things in their rightful positions and respective priorities. They fear others will overtake their worldly sheep and forget that God has promised that the inheritance of the heathen will be for the righteous. I wish we know our stand in the Lord like David did.

Second, God may want you to climb to the top of the mountain and then down to the other side. That is victory, but it costs a lot more strength and fresh air as you get short breaths while climbing; yet God is a very present help to you as you climb. He has allowed it and will be with you. This requires more patience, but the Lord will have come at the appointed time. It's at such times that you will need words like, "They that wait upon the Lord shall renew their strength." Though the vision will surely come, it may come slowly. Having read such words, you will have fed your computer (mind) well, and the Holy Spirit will switch on the retrieving button, and you will recall them. What will happen? You will overcome fear because you had your store full of the word of God. As you try to climb the mountain, there are times when you will fall and get hurt, and there will be enough medicine for you words such as, "Fear thou not, for I am with thee; be not dismayed for I am thy God; I will uphold thee with my right hand of righteousness" (Isaiah 41:10).

Just imagine falling down as you ascend that steep mountain and the Lord's right hand of righteousness upholding you. It is marvelous and wonderful. It is the word that brings victory over every fretting. "He gives power to the faint; and to them that have no might, He increases strength" (Isaiah 40:29). As you climb the mountain and are tempted to faint, the Lord continues to encourage you with such words. When your might is almost gone, He increases your strength. Yes, you lose your strength as you climb the high mountain, but praise be to our mighty God, who will be aware and come to your rescue to revive your strength.

One day as I was riding in a bus to work, one of the passengers almost fainted because the bus was full, and the air was stuffy. Before she fell, all passengers quickly opened the windows near them for fresh air to save this dear life of God's creation. Another sister near her began calling on the name of the Lord, and after some time, the woman revived and was given a seat. Later in the day, as I pondered that issue, the Holy Spirit quickened me and taught me a nice spiritual teaching. When we are almost fainting in our heavenly journey, God's angels are on hand, and they quickly use every available means in the spiritual storehouse of God to revive us again. One angel is busy opening the windows of heaven to give us wealth if we are fainting because of our lack of daily provisions. Another quickly opens the windows of healing if we are fainting because of sickness. Another offers a comfortable resting place so we can recover, and I tell you to date that I get encouraged by God's word, even as I have quoted it above. God won't just leave us without assistance when we are weary, but He will continue to renew our strength as we continue to wait on Him. Waiting on God is very different from waiting on a human being. Our colleagues may leave us at the last minute when we need them most, but God will never leave us or forsake us. As we wait on God in patience, climbing the mountains of life, we shall mount up with wings as eagles, running and not being weary, because our source of strength is surely from above. Climbing the mountains with the Lord is worth it all because we are on the winning side.

Third, God may literally remove the mountain so you may go through a smooth place to your spiritual destination. This is victory the Lord easily obtained for you, and it is not of yourself that you should boast. This is when you pray for something, and an answer is given quickly and directly. Be careful lest you regard yourself better than others who pray and wait for years before getting an answer, yet you prayed to the same God. All this success is from the word, because you can confidently claim whether you read before, "Behold, I will make thee a new sharp threshing instrument having teeth; thou shalt thresh the mountains and beat them small, and shalt make the hills as chaff, thou shalt fan them and the wind shall carry them away and the whirlwind shall scatter them and thou shalt rejoice in the Lord, and shalt glory in the holy one of Israel" (Isaiah 41:15–16).

As mentioned earlier, you will rejoice in the Lord and not in your own strength, since throughout these verses, we see it is the Lord's doing, not yours. You only used to witness the greatness of God and glorify Him among many people as you testify that if it weren't for the Lord, the mountain couldn't have been removed. Amen. Another reason we need to have the word of God dwelling richly in us is that because the devil always counts on every problem as a golden chance he can use to block our active service for God; and unless we are spiritually keen to apply the right word, he will always make us his victims.

God is with us just as He was with Abraham, our father of faith. "And the Lord appeared unto him the same night and said, I am the God of Abraham thy father; fear not for I am with thee and will bless thee, and multiply thy seed for my servant Abraham's sake" (Genesis 26:24). This was a time when Isaac was fretting about the Philistines, because they were envious of his prosperity. Previously, the herdsmen of Gerar had strived with him twice about the wells his servants had dug, but later we see that God made his enemies witness the hand of God being with him. "And they said, we saw certainly that the Lord was with thee; and we said; let there be now an oath betwixt us, even betwixt us and thee and let us make a covenant with thee" (Genesis 26:28). When we walk with the Lord boldly and righteously, He will make our enemies to be at peace with us and even desire to be in our company. They see the works of the God we believe in and trust. Therefore, it is vital to serve God fearlessly despite the many oppositions we might encounter because if God is with us, we shall always be the winners, and others will also desire to trust our God.

"Thou art now the blessed of the Lord" (v. 29). This confession came from the mouth of those who were against Isaac at first. Suppose he feared to dig another well. They couldn't witness the miracles of God in his life. Fear, as stated many times in this book, is a great

## Fear Not; God Is in Charge

menace that hinders God's move in the world today. From times immemorial, God has been looking for courageous people to do His work. Nevertheless, the devil is no respecter of persons because earlier Isaac cheated due to fear and said Rebecca wasn't his wife but his sister when the men of Gerar asked about his wife. "And Isaac dwelt in Gerar and the men of the place asked him of his wife and he said, she is my sister: for he feared to say she is my wife; lest, said he, the men of the place should kill me for Rebecca; because she was fair to look upon" (Genesis 26:6–7). Here we see the consequences of fearing when we are in the service of God. Isaac's possessiveness of his wife made him fear. It's good not to be so possessive because so much possessiveness makes us forget the divine protection of our God. Isaac thought he could be killed because of his wife, yet the God of Israel was His watchman who never slumbers.

When we cling so much to worldly things, we lose the anointing from God because we almost adore them. Rebecca's beauty made Isaac fear, leading him to cheat. Later Abimelech, king of the Philistines, knew Rebecca wasn't Isaac's sister when he watched from a window as Isaac sported with her (v. 8). He called Isaac to him and inquired to know the truth. The God of divine protection had already taken care of Isaac's fear. "And Abimelech said, what is this thou hast done unto us? one of the might lightly have lien with thy wife, and shouldest have brought guiltiness upon us. And Abimelech charged all his people, saying; he that toucheth this man or his wife shall surely be put to death" (vv. 10–11). God used the king to show Isaac that He cared for him. Isaac feared mere men, but God used men in higher powers as his bodyguards.

In the same way, many times we fear very minor things as far as our able God is concerned, which God takes care of from a very high perspective, even without our knowledge like in this case of Isaac. If God be for us, who can be against us? Nobody so long as we obey God and keep His commandments. He will always be with us, just as He was with Abraham.

Our God provides when we obey. Another reason we shouldn't fear is because our God provides everything we need. The word is the key to getting what we need. The Bible gives us several instances when God provided for His own, and He has never changed because He is the same yesterday, today, and forever. See 1 Kings 17:13–14. This widow had reached her dead end, but God intervened with a "Fear not" through His servant Elijah. This whole chapter is full of encouragement the Lord provided through unexpected sources. All Elijah told the woman to do was obey, and she hearkened, unlike many these days who are always giving reasons instead of acting on the voice of God. "And she went and did according to the saying of Elijah; and she and her house did eat many days" (v. 15). Trusting and obeying God are the keys to opening and closing every door as need be. As she obeyed, she received enough for that particular day and more days later (many days).

Previously in this chapter, we see that God had already provided a source of supply for His servant. "Thou shalt drink of the brook: and I have commanded the ravens to feed thee there" (v. 4). This to human beings could have been an unexpected source, but God used it for His glory. The fact that the ravens of all the creatures were commanded to feed His servant may be unreasonable, and Elijah had all the reasons to question God, but he obeyed because he knew God wasn't a man that lies. So he just acted in obedience. "So he went and did according unto the word of the Lord" (v. 5). He never doubted God but acted at His holy voice.

Today the devil holds firmly to a very strong tool to hinder God's blessings on His people: doubt. With doubt, you can never receive anything from God since you will just do for the sake of trying without faith, and the word clearly says that a double-minded person will receive nothing from the Lord. Building our faith is the only weapon of fighting doubt, and the only way to build the same is by reading the word of God, which is His voice to us. Faith is the hand that takes God's promises as contained in His holy word. It is only when we have faith that we can please God and ourselves since we shall have peace as we know His promises are yea and amen.

The outcome of Elijah's obedience to God was wonderful, and it can be the same for us if we choose to obey. "And the ravens brought

## Fear Not; God Is in Charge

him bread and flesh in the evening and he drank from the brook" (v. 6). His daily needs were met because he obeyed without questioning. It was God's work to provide, and Elijah was simply to hearken and obey. Even when the brook dried because of drought, God knew and had prepared another means of supplying His servant's very needs of life through a widow. When our supply dries up, the Lord is always aware, and He always has some other means to meet our everyday needs.

There is an old widow near where I reside, and many times God has used her to meet my needs through her generosity. Once, I had visitors, and I had already begun preparing them plain black coffee since I didn't have money to buy milk. I heard a knock at the door and opened it. The widow greeted us and brought me two bottles of milk; she reasoned that she had always wanted to come by, but time had been against her. Time was her excuse, but God had wanted it that way so He could meet my need at the most needed hour. God provides for His own, even more than we expect.

Another day after work, I wanted to buy green maize, but my money wasn't sufficient for all the commodities I urgently required. I decided to stop buying maize since there was something else we could cook instead, although I missed the dish. Reaching home, I met that same widow, who had brought maize. I was excited to see how God honors the desires of His servants. He always keeps a record of all our desires and needs, and He is always ready to meet them as we commit our lives fully to Him. This wasn't a problem but a desire. What a mighty God we serve, who is so considerate even to our unprayed-for desires. Commit your ways to the Lord, and He shall meet your heart's desires. Fear not, my ally, because even today God is still providing when our sources of supply dry up by preparing a widow to meet your needs. It may not be through a widow, since God's ways aren't like ours, but be assured that another source of supply is being prepared when the current one dries up. Many times I have seen God provide through miraculous ways and channels, but I have shared these two because they were specifically met through a widow like in the case of Elijah.

All we need to do is trust God in patience since we know He is never late or too early, but He always intervenes at the right time.

Waiting on God patiently always pays without any regrets. It helps us to fight anxiety and obey God. There is no other way to be happy in the Lord than to trust and obey Him like this man Elijah did. The devil makes us fret over many things, and even our worrying can do nothing except add more problems on top of already-existing ones, such as depression, ulcers, continuous anger, hatred, suspicion, and so forth. On our own, we can do nothing without the Lord helping us. When we are heavy laden, God comprehends, and that's why we are always being called to His rest, which no worldly friend can provide. "I have commanded a widow woman there to sustain thee" (v. 9). The word *there* can teach us many things. Out there in isolation, out there without a job, out there while waiting for a spouse, out there waiting for a baby, out there as a divorcee—out there the list of all your needs may be endless, but God promises that *there* He has commanded a means of sustaining you.

This widow might not have been famous, but God prepared her to meet the needs of His servant. You may also not be famous, even in your church, but if God has prepared you, you will be used to meet the needs of a very important person in the service of God. Be careful, lest you miss this wonderful chance due to an inferiority complex syndrome. God doesn't always work with recognized or famous people because He is a God of encouraging the low-esteemed lots. In chapter one, I shared in detail the many lowly people God used, and even today, He hasn't changed. When God sends you on a stony path, He always provides strong shoes to bear the sharp stones that could easily hurt you. Therefore, fear not. Elijah's problems created a long-term solution for this particular widow. It was his problems God met, and He further expanded His hand on her just like the saying "killing many birds with one stone." It may sound funny to us as human beings, but God's ways and plans aren't like ours, but they are the best ones for us. The drought came so God could send Elijah to this particular widow and meet her needs because of her obedience. Obedience as we live in this world is vital and opens ways of God's blessings to us and even to others.

Elijah obeyed to go when God talked to him. The widow obeyed

## Fear Not; God Is in Charge

when Elijah instructed her to make a morsel for him. Suppose this woman was so possessive, as mentioned earlier. She could have argued that it wasn't realistic to finish all she had and take the risk at the word of this servant of God. The devil has invented a language of "You can't take a risk," and many use these words, which have hindered many blessings just because people don't want to lose. Christ stated clearly that he who loses his life will save it, but he who saves it will lose it. When we lose by obeying God, we gain because we receive many blessings from the Lord. When we fast, we lose physically, but spiritually we gain, and others still gain as we pray for them. When we go out to serve God, we lose the company of our dear ones, but we gain spiritually because in our absence, God keeps blessing us as He provides for our daily needs. Others still gain as they hear the gospel and get healed, delivered, uplifted, and saved. Losing physically brings gains in many ways and to many people. As we strive in prayers, pulling down the strongholds of the enemy, we gain spiritually, and the world at large gains as we intercede for rulers, kings, and the body of Christ at large while we pray for other saints and church leaders.

Abraham obeyed, and God provided a ram for a burnt offering instead of his only son, whom he loved, Isaac. He decided to take the risk of sacrificing his only son because of the voice of God, the giver. Genesis 22. This chapter is full of Abraham's obedience to God.

First, God called Abraham, and he responded, "Behold here I am" (v. 1). Many are being called, but they don't respond. They just disobey due to some things they value that they feel they cannot forsake to obey God (they don't want to take the risk). Since creation, God has been calling mankind to repentance, and many have been hiding like Adam in the midst various sins as they give God conditions, forgetting their entire lives are under His full control. After Abraham responded, God gave him instructions. "Take now thy son, thine only son Isaac whom thou loveseat, and get thee into the land of Moorish and offer him there for a burnt offering upon one of the mountains which I will tell thee of" (v. 2).

This was a hard request, but Abraham obeyed God. It doesn't matter how hard a thing may be so long as God tells you to do it.

He already knows the hardness, value, and effect; and He has the power to give us enough grace to bear the repercussions of the same. Isaac was born in old age through God's power, yet God later required him for a burnt offering. He was making more channels of blessing Abraham and many other nations through him. We read, "And I will make thee exceeding fruitful, and I will make nations of thee, and kings shall come out of thee" (Genesis 17:6). God required Abraham's obedience by demanding his very best and the only son. God to date requires the best from us, not just the leftovers many give. What you value most is what God wants to use to bless you and others if only you obey His words and commandments. God had earlier told Abraham, "Walk before me and be thou perfect" (17:1). Being perfect calls us to be obedient in all things, and then God will do good things in our lives. God required Abraham to leave his normal residential environment when offering this precious gift on a mountain. For God to meet us in a mighty way, we need to leave our normal residences and isolate ourselves so we can be completely attentive to Him alone without other voices disturbing those surrounding us. Just imagine if he was to offer Isaac in the house or around the homestead. His wife, Sarah, might have missed him for some time, and, looking for him, she could have hindered God's will by rebuking her husband.

God was aware of all these things, and hence He advised Abraham to go far to a mountain, which He directed him to. As Abraham went, he took two of his young men (servants) together with his son, Isaac, the target of the whole ceremony. The location was far since it was after three days that he saw the place afar off. We note that Abraham reached the place and left his servants behind and went with only his son to worship, but he promised them to return. We are also required to leave some companies when we seek God on a mountain so God can meet us individually and not in a multitude. He always lets people hear His voice individually. Isaac wondered what type of a sacrifice it could be without a lamb and asked his father, "Behold the fire and the wood, but where is the lamb for a burnt offering is?" (22:7). Our thoughts and humanity may pose such questions to our unshakable

## Fear Not; God Is in Charge

faith, but we should be confident in our God like Abraham. who replied by faith to his son, "My son, God will provide himself a lamb for a burnt offering" (v. 8).

God had already specified to Abraham that He wanted him to offer Isaac as an offering, but He didn't reveal this detail to him. Why not? He couldn't just reveal the secret between Him and God because Isaac could obviously and violently run for his life. Many times people miss the blessings of God because of carelessly revealing to other people, whom they regard as best friends, what was meant to be only between them and God. The best friend is God, who keeps your secrets. The devil can use anybody to contaminate the anointing of a particular message, which God wanted you to handle as an individual without letting it out. This is what Abraham did, and we see the end outcome that surely God provided as Abraham had told his son.

Hannah also kept her prayer details to herself, even when Eli misunderstood her. "And it came to pass as she continued praying before the Lord that Eli marked her mouth. Now Hannah spake in her heart; only her lips moved but her voice was not heard; therefore Eli thought she was drunken" (1 Samuel 1:12–13). Her being misunderstood never bothered her business with God of praying. She continued without fear. Many times today we will be misunderstood to be fools, but that shouldn't bother us since we know the one we are following. Look unto Him alone, and all will be well. Being misunderstood by close friends makes us fret, even to the extent of giving up our faith. Fear not; you are more than a conqueror with Christ. The devil normally brings these things so we reveal our secrets with God to the wrong people, and in the process, we miss the goal of the whole event. May God help us to be wise in our spiritual journey, which is being fought by many.

Eli provoked her more, which could have made her angrily drain out all she was praying for, but thank God she was stable in her faith in God. "And Eli said unto her, how long wilt thou be drunken? Put away thy wine from thee" (1 Samuel 1:14). This was an open channel for Hannah to disclose all she was praying for in defense, but she regarded God to be her defense. She had a personal hassle, which she could share only with God and no other earthly friend, not even her husband. She left home to go to the temple to pray. We also need to leave our homes and go to the house of God for our very personal burdens like this woman did. She purposed to seek God and not man and didn't even ask the priest to pray for her (v. 10). God, who is a rewarder of those who diligently seek Him, rewarded her with a baby, and everybody in the family saw the fruits of her secret prayers. When we seek God secretly, He will answer us, and our blessings will be witnessed by many and glorify God. God had closed her womb, creating a circumstance for her to pray to Him secretly, and He answered her.

Even today God still closes doors in our lives as He awaits someone to pray so He opens them for His glory. What if you seek advice from others, whom you regard as counselors or best friends? You might miss the plan of God. Fear not as you seek God because He is able to design and fit the key and unlock the mysteries in our lives without any assistance of our earthly friends. He is ever ready to respond to the prayers of the saints in times of need. Why fear if you are one of the saints? If you are not, this is your chance to become a saint by accepting Christ as your Savior and hence giving you power to become a child of God (John 1:12).

Man couldn't comfort Hannah's problem, because even when her husband tried to, she was still sorrowful and looking to God alone to console her. "Am I not better to thee than ten sons" (v. 8). Her husband tried to comfort her, but all was a futile attempt without God. Many times we need God's touch and comfort, not the touch of any earthly person. Therefore, we have a responsibility to let God know our sorrows, and He will always answer. Ask, and you'll get. Seek, and you'll find. Knock, and the door will be opened. God doesn't hassle to meet our needs, but the hassle is always with us by not going to Him in prayer. It's never too late. You can start now, and He is very ready to start acting on your every need. God, whom we seek, will reward us because He will be no man's debtor. Once we pray, we give God work, and He is efficient enough to complete everything we, His beloved children, assign to Him. If we don't give Him the work, He has no problem, but we always struggle on our own while He has freely volunteered to meet us at our very point of need when we pray.

Prayer is a direct line to call God, and it's never busy, unlike the worldly telephone lines. Sometimes I've found myself stuck as I try to ring people for vital purposes, only to find that the lines are engaged. I thank God that this heavenly line is never engaged. There is always an answer—with a yes, no, or wait—but they are all good enough answers to us from our maker. He provides even when we speculate the resources aren't there. He is Jehovah Jireh. What is that need you have now? Call to Him now, and He will answer you and show you great and hidden things that you know not. Yes, He will provide them. Our praying to God is just like placing an order, which is a step taken, and the next one is waiting for delivery. Yes, when we pray, we place our orders to God. He files our orders nicely, and at the right time, we see the delivery of whatever we needed. The delivery period may take some time, but it will always be accomplished. Therefore, we shouldn't allow the enemy to keep on placing unnecessary worries on our shoulders. We have an unfailing God and father, who is so dear to us. We need to testify to the devil openly that we have gone too far with our God to look back and worry. Why? God tells us, "Fear not, I am your God."

## God Gives Us Divine Protection

As mentioned earlier, insecurity is one of the reasons that brings fear. In God we have first-class security. One night I dreamed of seeing two rats under our bed. One was big, and the other was small. Looking at them, I saw one was dead, and the other was very weak. I removed them with a long stick. When we woke up, there were no lights, and we thought the problem was a normal power failure. As I left for work, I met one of our neighbors, who told me the meter box had been broken at night and a circuit breaker removed. At midday, God reminded me of what I had dreamed. In as much as those malefactors might have wanted to hurt us in our residence, we had super and first-class security in the Lord. As Christians, God doesn't just let us experience, dream, see, and hear things for the sake of them. I believe He always likes teaching us new things in what we can easily understand through our daily lives. The Bible clearly tells us that He who watches over us never sleeps or slumbers. That night He was awake and saw all that was happening. He protected us in a divine way.

Are you undergoing some kind of fear? God is a sure security who never fails and is free of charge. All you need to do is commit yourself to Him, and He will always be watching over your entire life. In times of danger, the Lord is our defense and says, "Touch not mine anointed, and do my people no harm" (Psalm 105:15). "Fear not, for they that be with us are more that they that be with them" (2 Kings 6:15). This was Elisha encouraging his servant who wasn't aware that they were under divine protection. This servant feared because he saw their city was surrounded by horses and chariots of the king of Samaria. He could only see with his eyes the chariots of their enemy. His inner eyes were closed, but thank God Elijah encouraged him. And Elisha prayed and said, "Lord, I pray thee, open his eyes, that he may see. And the Lord opened the eyes of the young man and he saw and behold, the mountain was full of horses and chariots of fire round about Elisha" (v. 17). Elisha never encouraged his servant by his own knowledge, but he sought the Lord in prayer. We shouldn't be encouraging the discouraged lot by our own power without prayers because prayer is the vision of the believer. It gives eyes to our faith. After he prayed, his servant's eyes were opened, and he saw in the spiritual realm that they who were with them were more than their foes. I get so encouraged because with God, we are always the majority.

My friend, if your spiritual eyes are open right where you are, you should know that you are under divine protection. It doesn't matter how many people are against you or how powerful their weapons are so long as you are with almighty God. He is a God of war. He fought for the Israelites, and He will fight for you too because He never changes. The weapons of our warfare are mighty through God. With God on our side, nobody can be against us. All we need to have is

## Fear Not; God Is in Charge

our spiritual eyes opened through prayer. Prayer is a divine key for you as a believer to use to open and close any doors the enemy closed to hinder your victory. It's the only answer to our daily confrontation with the enemy.

As we read the word, we realize prayer was more than part of Christ's life, and so we need it too as His followers and imitators for divine protection to be manifested. David also received divine protection when King Saul was after him because David had made God his security. He kept on trying. "And Saul sought him every day, but God delivered him not into his hands" (1 Samuel 23:14). God will never allow the enemy to trample His own. The enemy will try, but God's divine protection will be enough for us. David was a man of prayer; before his deliverance, he sought God, his protector, when he sensed danger. "Therefore David inquired of the Lord saying, Shall I go and smite these Philistines? And the Lord said unto David, go and smite the Philistines and save Keilah" (1 Samuel 23:2). He assumed the victory was his. He took a step to pray.

Many people today fail because they assume victory will just come. No, it won't just come; you need to pray, and God will intervene as per your prayers. We have our part, and God has His before we can see divine protection. Many Christians are very lazy about prayer, yet they expect God to protect them. Wake up and know that when we neglect private prayers, we remove ourselves from the focus of God's power. Many relax and complain that they have no time to pray, but for sure if you are determined, you will always have time for prayer. David was persistent in prayer, and so must we be. "Then David inquired of the Lord *yet again*. And the Lord answered him and said, Arise, go down to Keilah; for I will deliver the Philistines into thine hand" (1 Samuel 23:4, emphasis mine). He never prayed once the way many do; he sought God yet again continually. The outcome was protection from his enemy Saul, "but God delivered him not into his hand" (1 Samuel 23:14). That was divine protection. Pray again and again, and you'll be protected, because He who has promised is faithful to the very end.

When I was expecting my firstborn, I fell badly in our bathroom, and when I went to the hospital, the doctor said after a thorough checkup, "Woman, you are very lucky!" I knew I wasn't just lucky, but I was blessed and under divine protection—and my unborn kid as well. John was thrown into the sea of Patmos to die, but God told him, "Fear not … And he laid his right hand upon me saying unto me; 'Fear not, I am the first and the last'" (Revelation 1:17). This was a wonderful time, chance, and experience of God touching him with His right hand. He continued to build his confidence in Him by revealing Himself to John that He was the first and the last. Our God isn't just like any other person, who is there at the genesis of a problem and not there at its terminus. He will see you through from the beginning to the very end. His divine protection is 100 percent.

I see the entire solution of not fearing in the image of a nail. You can't just strike a nail once and claim to have completed the work. You need to strike it time and again until the nailhead is completely in line with the level of your service. Reading the word of God and praying have to be done time and again until they are completely applicable to our situations and hence bring success and deliver us from fear. If you put a bottle full of maize, nicely corked, in the midst of hens, you'll observe a very nice game. They will struggle to bite the bottle, expecting to reach the maize, but all will be a futile attempt. Why? They can see the maize, but the bottle prevents them.

When we accept the Lord to save us, He covers us with His precious blood. Since we are in the world, the enemy will see us, but, coming to attack us, he struggles to no avail when we are fully covered by the blood of Jesus, which is our security fence. The danger comes when one lives a dual life with compromise because that's just like putting the maize in a broken bottle on one side; obviously it will be accessible to the attacks of the hens. The same case, dual Christianity, paves ways for the enemy to interfere with your life. It's no wonder one singer sang, "I am gonna hide right under the blood where the devil can do me no harm." We need to hide completely and not just partly in the blood of Jesus, and then you will experience divine protection. Divine protection is yours for the asking; all you need to do is meet the conditions needed.

# Chapter 9

# **Overcoming Inner Fear**

WE CAN OVERCOME inner fear by having the word of God inside our lives and praying the same words, which is very effective. God always hastens to perform His word, and if you read it and then pray, reminding Him of what He promised, inner fear will have no place in your life. "Then said the Lord unto me, thou hast well seen: for I will hasten my word to perform it" (Jeremiah 1:12). All is ours for the asking because God isn't a man that He should lie or repent of His promises to us as His children, whom He purchased with the precious blood of His Son, Jesus Christ. When we know our rights and position in the word of God, we easily overcome fear. The word says we have been given power, authority, and the keys of the kingdom of God.

When Peter confidently identified Christ as the Son of the living God, Christ, he realized not through flesh and blood but through his Father in heaven, who had revealed it to him. Jesus told Peter He would build on that rock His church, which the gates of hell wouldn't prevail against. He gave him the keys of the kingdom of heaven, promising that whatever he bound here on earth, it would be bound even in heaven. As Christians, when we confidently recognize Christ as the Son of the living God by letting Him rule over our entire lives, the same promises Jesus gave automatically become ours. As in the case of Peter, it can never be through flesh and blood but through spiritual revelation like in the time of Nicodemus.

Authority is the legal power or right delegated to somebody. Therefore, as Christians God has already delegated power to us through His Son, Jesus Christ, as we live under the sun over every other power of the enemy, the devil.

Policemen have authority from their respective governments delegated to them. They represent their respective governments wherever they are. For example, traffic police have the mandate to stop any vehicle irrespective of its good or poor make or its senior or high-ranked owner. No vehicle owner can ignore any traffic rule or order and escape the laid-down penalty if at all justice is practiced without corruption and bribery. The policemen have the mandate delegated to them by the government. We have authority as Christians even more than that of the policemen delegated to us by Jesus Christ if at all we trust in Him as our Lord and Savior. Therefore, we have all the mandate to stop the enemy poking into our lives. It doesn't matter what our calibers are so long as we are born-again Christians. To explain further, let me give a good example.

An office manager who is a born-again Christian has the mandate over his or her boss's mistreatments or underpinnings because Christ has delegated the higher power from above to this particular manager. Nevertheless, this is only if prayer is made and a claim of God's promises from His word in prayer. Christians, we have a reason to live joyfully, peacefully, prosperous lives and so forth if we know our rightful positions in the kingdom of God. The only hassle we have today is our failing to know our rightful positions in the kingdom of God, and the enemy has tried all he can to make us ignorant; hence we fail to know our rights in the word of God. Let us wake up, search the scriptures, and live the way God expects us to.

The Bible clearly tells us we are peculiar people.

> But ye are a chosen generation, a royal priesthood, an holy nation, a peculiar people; that ye should show

## Fear Not; God Is in Charge

forth the praises of him who hath called you out of darkness into his marvelous light. (1 Peter 1:9)

For thou art an holy people unto the Lord thy God: the Lord thy God hath chosen thee to be a special people unto Himself, above all people that are upon the face of the earth. (Deuteronomy 7:6)

From these texts, we should know God has chosen us for a very good reason. When we choose something, it's always among many other things; therefore, God has also chosen us out of very many people with a purpose. The way we can choose to buy a good and expensive dress from a shop only to keep it inside a wardrobe without use is the same way God can deal with us. We haven't been chosen to stay cold, desperate, sorrowful, poor, idle, and so forth. It's for a special day that we buy a nice and expensive dress and put it on. So in the same way, God has chosen us for a special ministry or purpose for His glory. We have also not been chosen to do only the normalities of our respective traditions but to do the extraordinary the way Jesus did, even if we will violate the traditions of men, which at times make the word of God to be of no effect. No wonder Paul was always cautioning people on such behaviors.

Jesus used to heal the sick on the Sabbath day, which violated the traditions of men, but He preferred to please God rather than man. We need to do all for the glory of God. Friends, we also need to be merciful to the desperate lots who have been forsaken in our societies, even if our traditions don't allow for them, but we had better obey God than man. Speaking in tongues is normally forbidden in some of our churches, but let us be careful to do what the Bible says than what our church says or believes. God has also chosen us to be above all people on the face of the earth. Frankly speaking, the devil has completely interchanged these scriptures, and many Christians have become his followers; hence, they are always below unbelievers. This situation isn't right biblically. The word of God is true. It is time we tell the devil point blank that we have known the truth of who we are and need to take our rightful positions. Stop suffering now as a child of God and claim the promises of God.

Are you sick now? The Lord wants you whole because He was wounded for your sins; He received thirty-nine strokes for all your ailments, sickness, and so forth. Every stroke he received, I believe, removed every ailment you would normally have now. Claim your healing now so you can manage to serve God in whatever area He needs you. Our fields should be the most productive because God said so in Deuteronomy 28:11–12. "And the Lord shall make thee plenteous in goods in the fruit of thy ground, in the land in the fruit of the cattle and in the fruit of thy ground in the land which the Lord swear unto thy fathers to give thee. The Lord shall open unto thee his good treasure, the heaven to give the rain unto thy land in his season and to bless all the work of thine hands; and thou shalt lend unto many nations and thou shalt not borrow."

No, we aren't beggars, and we should never be if all is always well with our God. Lack of the word of God in our lives just brings hazards. Why should you be a beggar? The word clearly says you should be the one to give not only to beggars but also to the nations. God's vision is always a world vision in His mind. We shouldn't be narrow minded. Go beyond your family members, tribe, and nation; and reach out to the regions beyond, to the entire world. But remember, all these won't just come without a price. The price is, "Hearken unto the Lord and obey Him in all ways." As said many times in this book, for every promise of God, there is always a condition to be met. Joshua 1:8 is the condition we need to meet for success always and in all things. "This book of the law shall not depart out of thy mouth: but thou shalt meditate there in day and night that thou mayest observe to do according to *all that is written* therein: for then thou shalt make thy way prosperous and then thou shalt have good success" (emphasis added).

Some Christians have a habit of believing and obeying only some words of the Bible, but I caution you that for any good success, you should be obedient to *all that is written*. We are "peculiar people"; we particularly belong to God, and therefore, we have all the right over every force that exalts itself over the knowledge of Christ. We also have the keys of the kingdom of heaven. Keys open and lock where necessary. You can lock a room with good things, and you also have the right to open the same realistically. Spiritually, this is what we have been promised. So why should we just hold the key to open that door of employment the devil has been locking for so long? You also have the key to get that healing the devil has been blocking by making you always sickly. You have the key to open that door of prosperity the devil has been locking by always making you poor and needy. It's time we tell the devil face-to-face that we've had enough of his tricks. He has been misusing our keys by snatching them from us and locking all the good things our heavenly Father has been wanting us to possess. These keys were snatched sometimes when we held them carelessly and in idleness, but now we know our rights.

"And from the days of John the Baptist until now, the kingdom of God suffereth violence, and the violent take it by force" (Mathew 11:12). The days, friends, of pleading with our foe are no more. We need to be violent against his devices and get back what he has been withholding from us. He has stolen our joy, yet the joy of the Lord is our strength; and hence, leaving us weak spiritually, we need to take it back violently. I've never seen policemen pleading with a violent robber; they give orders, and if those aren't obeyed, the result brings consequences of either murder or bullets fired in the air, which also scare the surrounding environs. We need to give the devil orders now and demand that he return what rightfully belongs to us. Our health has been stolen, and we are always sickly or on medicines that obviously drain our pockets, yet it's God's will that we be healthy to enable us to serve Him effectively. We need to violently take back our health now from the devil. He has stolen our joy in marriage, and now there seems to be another philosophy that marriage can never be in harmony throughout, yet from the beginning, God made them, man and woman, one and for fellowship and company. We need our marriage harmony back from the enemy since he has made us to believe opposite of what God intended us to be. Our prosperity has been stolen, yet Christ became poor that we may be rich. The enemy has cheated us to believe for so long that we need to be poor here on earth to be rich in heaven. If there is a time when we need to be rich, it is when we are here on earth materially so we can reach the unreached with the gospel of Jesus Christ. God has from time immemorial wanted us to be above all nations in every way: spiritually, physically, materially, and mentally. It is when we are rich all round that we shall be able to lend and not borrow.

> And all the people of the earth shall see that thou art called by the name of the Lord; and they shall be afraid of thee. And the Lord shall make thee plenteous in goods, in the fruit of thy body, and in the fruit of thy cattle, and in the fruit of thy ground, in the land which the Lord swear unto thy fathers to give thee. The Lord shall open unto thee his good treasure, the heaven to give the rain unto thy land in his season and bless all the work of thine hand: and thou shalt lend unto many nations, and thou shalt not borrow. And the Lord shall make thee the head, and not the tail; and thou shalt be above only, and thou shalt not be beneath: if that thou hearken unto the commandments of the Lord thy God, which I command thee this day, to observe to do them. (Deuteronomy 28:10–13)

- Spiritually rich in the things of God
- Mentally rich in education, skills, sound mind, and wisdom
- Physically rich in health and materials

These three types of riches are vital because it's the spiritually rich, mentally rich, and physically rich who can effectively share the gospel worldwide with every nation and different languages without any hindrances. The devil always has a technique of misquoting the word of God to suit his tactics of misleading the uninformed Christian. He did it to Jesus after He had fasted for forty days and forty

## Fear Not; God Is in Charge

nights, but Jesus told the devil three different times, "It is written." I thank God that Christ had the word dwelling richly in Him so He was able to get the right word for Satan. You need the same word dwelling richly in you so you can give the devil the right word for every move he makes before you with an imitated word for his selfish purposes of getting you away from the plan of God.

"And this gospel of the kingdom shall be preached in all the world for a witness unto all nations; and then shall the end come" (Matthew 24:14). I have traveled to different parts of our country for missions, and in one way or another there is always the hindrance of a language barrier, which is normally combated by interpretation to the understandable language. So the interpreter needs to know either English or Swahili, from which he or she then interprets that particular regional language. Imagine illiterate people taking the gospel to the regions beyond. There would always be an obstacle because of the communicating languages, which is gotten rid off only by our being educated.

Once, I managed to go to Switzerland for missions, and the greatest hassle was communication. We had only one person, our host, who knew English and could interpret into their national language, German. At times he was extremely tired, but the grace of God was enough. What I am endeavoring to impress is the need for every Christian to be mentally rich, to be multilingual. If some of us had been when we went to Switzerland, we would have easily combated the problem of the language barrier, and hence our host, the only interpreter we had, wouldn't have been so burdened. So by all means, effective preachers need to be educated enough, and we also should learn other languages if we plan to reach the entire world effectively, because our vision should be to reach the uttermost parts of the world. People who do this should be skillful enough, and I thank God that we have such people in the Bible, even as we read, "And the king spake unto Ashpenaz the master of his eunuchs, that he should bring certain of the children of Israel and the king's seed, and of the princes: children in whom was no blemish, but well favored and skillful in all wisdom and cunning in knowledge and understanding science and such as had ability in them to stand in the king's palace and whom they might teach the learning and the tongue of the Chileans" (Daniel 1:3–4).

In this text, we see that Daniel and his colleagues had all three types of riches, and hence they were chosen. We still need such people in the churches to enable effective preaching. Days are gone, friends, when the devil used to teach that the most educated were normally far from Christianity. Education should be our gateway to reaching many for the kingdom. Are you misusing your education? Arise now and glorify God with that skill you have, and you will be blessed abundantly.

"Let the word of Christ dwell in you richly in all wisdom, teaching and admonishing one another in psalms and hymns and spiritual songs singing with grace in your hearts to the Lord" (Colossians 3:16). Since the gospel of the kingdom is to be preached everywhere as Christ commanded His disciples, of whom we are today, we need to have the word of God dwelling richly in us, and the Holy Spirit will quicken the word as we go to minister. The word also admonishes us to be able to answer every question from one who is thirsting for the salvation as you preach. Spiritual richness gives us a burden to serve the Lord as He expects from us. "How sweet are thy words unto my taste! yea, sweeter than honey to my mouth! Through thy precepts I understand: therefore I hate every false way. Thy word is a lamp unto my feet, and a light unto my path" (Psalms 119:103–105).

Being rich in the word of God, you can easily counsel somebody who may have been wayward as a cult member. He or she tells you what he or she believes, and without a word, you can search your Bible for a relevant scripture, but you can't get it because the devil is very keen to hide the scriptures, even from those for whom you have known their whereabouts for years. Jesus Himself had the word of God dwelling richly in Him, and when the devil tempted Him three times, He quoted the scriptures as we see recorded in Luke 4, telling the devil, "It is written."

"And the devil said unto him. If thou be the son of God, command this stone that it be made bread. And Jesus answered him, saying, It is

## Fear Not; God Is in Charge

written, that man shall not live by bread alone but by every word of God" (vv. 3–4). Suppose this command were directed to you. Which scripture would you quote to the devil? Be keen to have the word of God richly dwelling in you because there is always a word for every situation you go through.

"And the devil said unto him, all this power will I give thee, and the glory of them: for that is delivered unto me; and to whosoever I will give it, if thou therefore will worship me, all shall be thine. And Jesus answered and said unto him, get thee behind me Satan for it is written, thou shalt worship the Lord thy God, and him only shalt thou serve" (vv. 6–9). So many Christians these days are power hungry, and I try to imagine, if this were offered to them, that they would have hardly remembered to inquire whether it was the will of God, let alone quoting a scripture. What is your response when chances of quick riches come to you, dear brethren? Even Christians can be victims of deceit if they are after getting riches more than pleasing their maker. As referenced in 2 Kings 5:20-27, there was consequences when Gehazi, Elisha's servant, decided to take advantage of what Elisha had given up on for the sake of maintaining his integrity.

"And he brought him to Jerusalem and set him on a pinnacle of the temple, and said unto him, if thou be the son of God, cast thyself down from hence: for it is written, He shall give his angels charge over thee, to keep thee: and in their hands they shall bear thee up, lest at any time thou dash thy foot against a stone. And Jesus answering said unto him, It is said thou shalt not tempt the Lord thy God" (vv. 9–12). Being imitators of Jesus Christ, we definitely need to have the word of God dwelling richly in us, just as He did. Please also note that Christ hadn't beforehand prepared these scriptures He gave the devil, but He had them treasured in his heart.

Do you treasure the word of God in you? Start learning the Bible now lest you be a victim of the enemy. The devil knows the Bible from Genesis to Revelation but for the wrong motive. Have the word richly dwelling in you for your protection. When this devil comes with a mere word to victimize you, apply the Bible rightly since the devil is always tricky. If Jesus hadn't known how to apply the word rightly, each time the devil confronted Him, The devil could have created a chance for Jesus to sin against His maker.

> And the lord will take away from thee all sickness, and will put none of the evil disease of Egypt, which thou knowest upon thee; but will lay them upon all them that hate thee. (Deuteronomy 7:15)

> But thou shalt have a perfect and just weight, a perfect and just measure shalt have: that thy days may be lengthened in the land which the Lord thy God gives thee. (Deuteronomy 25:15)

I'm sure many Christians don't know that being overweight is unbiblical if it affects their service for God, whereby they can hardly walk long distances, especially in missionary work. That's why we need to be very rich in the word of God. Sicknesses of all kinds have also been promised to be removed from us. This means they are within us, but once we obey God, He removes or take them away from us. I wonder how we can glorify God if we go for a particular mission. All of us have severe headaches and stomachaches, even to the extent of bending down and holding our stomachs and heads as we tell people to come to Jesus so they will find joy. This presentation would be a total contradiction, and I believe sinners would prefer to be where they are as they regard themselves better off without the sickness. We can easily make the word of God of no effect because of failing to know our rights in the word.

"And to make thee high above all nations which he hath made, in praise, and in name, and in honor; and that thou mayest be an holy people unto the Lord thy God, as he hath spoken" (Deuteronomy 26:19). All these different texts show us the need of our being rich health wise and material wise for effective ministering. Material riches enable us to provide to the poor we preach to, and they need food, clothes, and so forth. I have gone for some missions, and when altar calls are made, people in torn clothes obey the word; it's a shame to

## Fear Not; God Is in Charge

take them to church that way. In many cases, clothes of missionaries are given to these newly born converts. Therefore, it's vital to have material riches when spreading the gospel. Suppose each missionary had only two sets of clothes for himself or herself. How would the missionary help people who come to the Lord naked, dirty, and so forth? A beggar cannot preach to another beggar effectively, but if he or she is first delivered from the situation, then the word will be very effective, and he or she will desire to come to your side to be like you.

"And that you study to be quiet and to do your own business and to work with your own hands as we command you that ye may walk honestly toward them that are without and that you may lack nothing" (1 Thessalonians 4:11–12). Studying and working hard will give us riches, and we won't lack daily provisions to hinder our reaching more souls for Christ unless God allows it purposely to teach us something, because all things work together for good to those who love the Lord. Idleness is a self-inflicted curse, and some people are misled by the enemy as they misquote the word to suit their laziness.

Come on and work hard. Our God is a hard-working God, and I wonder whom you can resemble if you go idling about while you claim that they who preach should eat of the gospel if you aren't a full-time pastor or minister under a particular home church. Paul knew well that as an apostle, the Thessalonians brethren ought to have supported him, but he was always eager to comment. "For neither at any time used we flattering words, as ye know, nor a cloak of covetousness; God is a witness nor of men sought we glory, neither of you nor yet of others, when we might have been burdensome as the apostles of Christ but we were gently among your, even as a nurse cherisheth her children" (1 Thessalonians 2:5–7). As apostles, they had the right for these brethren in Thessalonica to support them, but they preferred to be independent for the glory of God. It's not a sin to be a minister of God and still do your work lest you be a burden to the people you are serving. It's still good to be a full-time minister, but I think it's best when you are working—not just because you are paid but because you know whom you have believed.

Some people who cover their laziness opt to regard themselves as full-time workers yet not under a particular home church. May God help us to see that we are hardworking servants of the most high God and not just serving God full-time because we have nothing else to do. As we proceed in the service of God, whether full-time or part-time, we need to be confident that God has promised that He will never leave us or forsake us. "But now thus saith the lord that created thee, o Jacob, and he that formed thee, o Israel *fear not*, for I have redeem thee; thou art mine. When thou passest through the waters, I will be with thee; and through the rivers, they shall not overflow thee: when thou walkest through the fire, thou shalt not be burned; neither shall the flame kindled upon you. For I am the lord thy God, the holy one of Israel, thy savior. I gave Egypt for thy reason, Ethiopia and Seba for thee" (Isaiah 43:1–3, emphasis added).

We are so valuable before God, and we should be confident that what He promises us He will bring to pass because He isn't a man that He should lie. What is it that you are fearing while God says to you, "Fear not"? What is that watery way you are passing through while He says to you, "The waters shall not overflow you"? What is that fire you are in while He says, "You shall not be burned neither the flame kindle upon you"? It is always good to take the word of God in its simplicity without any addition or subtraction if we are to live while experiencing our authority in Him. "For I testify unto every man that heareth the words of the prophesy of this book, if any man shall add unto these things God shall add unto him the plagues that are written in this book and if any man shall take away from the words of the book of this prophesy, God shall take away his part out of the book of life and out of the holy city and from the things which are written in this book" (Revelation 22:18–19). Failing to take God at His word is taking away from this book of the prophecy, the Bible, yet His promises are yea and amen. Our authority and keys will depend on our obedience to the word of God. It's worth it all for us Christians to know that the gospel is not only a program for action but also a proclamation of the power at our disposal.

Since the source of what makes us fret in our lives is supernatural, we need supernatural weapons to combat it: the word and prayer.

## Fear Not; God Is in Charge

It's when we pray that God enters the supernatural problem with His supernatural wisdom and power, enabling us to hold onto His words "Fear not." We can never overcome fear by experience but only by daily submitting to the Lord and His words through prayers, which are an effective spiritual weapon. Our titles are immaterial in this field, and that is why we see even reverends, pastors, and so forth becoming prey of the enemy through immorality, corruption, forgery, and so forth just because they are ignorant of the devil's devices. You can never assume things of the devil and succeed to overcome inner fear. Assumptions are an open channel to make the devil a winner against you. As the devil bombards us with discouragement, we must be very ready, holding our sword of the spirit (the word) to fight him back and hence overcome inner fear. An empty-handed soldier is an obvious victim to defeat, and in the same way, any Christian soldier who lacks the word, by which he can tell the devil he is a defeated fellow, will only end up with more fear than when he went to the battlefield with the enemy (the devil).

In defeating inner fear, we have our part to carry the right spiritual tools, and God has His part to fulfill our desires through those tools when applied correctly. You may go to a shamba (garden) with the right tools and fail to dig. How? If you don't take the right action while embarking on your mission, you may have the word and fail to apply it; then you would have only yourself to blame for the defeat. God will always work on our initiative; for example, He will answer us when we pray, give us the desires of our hearts when we commit our ways to Him, open the doors when we knock, bless the work of our hands when we really work with our hands, beautify our feet when we take the gospel out, heal the sick when we lay our hands on them, and so forth.

When he obeyed Christ's word "Come," Peter walked on water. That was faith. In the middle of the sea, he closed his spiritual eyes and opened his physical ones, and he began to sink. Why? He ignored the initial word of Christ and endeavored to reason in his humanity. This tendency is very common in many Christians. We start the journey well with the Lord, trusting Him to see us through all life's obstacles, but immediately we start arguing realistically, we lose our vision, and hence fretting invades us. It's by faith, not by sight, and looking unto Jesus to deal with all the obstacles. Our role is just to obey and trust Him who has called us, and all the rest He will accomplish. As we look to God, many challenges will come, but we should be determined to press on toward the goal we have been summoned for.

My younger sister got married before I did because she was not saved and had no restrictions for a holy life whatsoever. I got married nine years later. There were many challenges and painful words, but I had known whom I had believed who at the right time gave me a husband. For all that period, I never gave up. I believe being busy for God contributed to my not being bothered with all the challenges. As is normally said, an idle mind is the devil's workshop; to manage the bombardment of the devil, you need to be busy for God, and I tell you, you will never regret it. The battle is worth it all. Once you are in business for God, He is always in your business, which booms in all dimensions with peace that no other normal business can give. There is joy because the joy of the Lord becomes your strength, life eternal awaits you in heaven, and Jehovah Jireh properly meets all your daily needs. All these overcome inner fear successfully.

Knowing where to take our bothers in life overcomes inner fretting as we have inner rest, and so when we hearken to the Lord, we shall manage. "Come unto me all ye that labor and are heavy laden, and I will give you rest" (Matthew 11:28). A heavy-laden person obviously has inner fear, wondering who can ever assist him or her. The Lord has volunteered to help you and me. All we must do is hearken to His call. Our obedience to God is to our own benefit, but if we ignore the help offered, we proceed, bearing burdens that worry us unnecessarily and foolishly. Once in my late pregnancy period, I entered a bus that lacked open seats, and I had to stand. I was so tired after just a short distance, not even a quarter of the way to my destination, and I regretted having boarded that bus. A man standing near me sensed my discomfort, touched one who was seated, and said, "*Si upatie huyu*

## Fear Not; God Is in Charge

*mama kiti tafadhali?*" (Can't you please give this lady a seat?). Looking at me with my protruding tummy, he woke up respectfully, and I sat down. I was so happy because somebody had at least offered me a seat to rest. What if he had offered the seat and I just stared at him? I would have seemed like the most idiotic person on earth to have refused a seat, yet I was tired. Christ is calling all who are frustrated, tired with life, yet many behave in such a foolish way as to refuse the rest the Lord offers. Please accept the rest now and give Him your life to save you, and all those inner fears you have will be taken care of. What needless pain you bear. Christ has offered to bear it all on your behalf.

Our daily needs often cause us to have inner fear, but God is good and always comprehends; and hence He continues to promise that He will meet with each of them. "But my God shall supply all your needs according to His riches in glory by Christ Jesus" (Philippians 4:19). God doesn't single them out, but He promises to meet *all*. So our trust in the Lord will easily overcome inner fear. The riches He will use are in glory, which to me means He will meet all in a very adequate way since He is all powerful. These are all to be met through Jesus, who acts like our bridge to reach God since mankind's fall in the Garden of Eden. My husband was jobless for seven and half months after a merger of the company he was working for, and doors of going out for missions were opened wider than ever before. Each mission required money, and I never missed a single one. Once, God talked to me and said He would provide what I needed to go where He sent me eight months before my husband lost his job. I trusted Him on every mission invitation I received and reminded Him of that promise to me as His child and servant. God, who is all knowing, had promised me this before the job ended so I could count Him faithful, and I continued to see His mighty hand. He provided in different ways and also at the eleventh hour.

One day I planned to go to a funeral for one of my cousins to minister in singing. My spirit was willing, but since I didn't have the money, I informed my husband that if I missed transport at the mortuary, I wouldn't proceed, but I had already asked permission from my place of work by faith. At the mortuary, I managed to get transport, and a friend of mine, who had my four hundred shillings, which I had given to her a long time ago, called me. She wasn't going but told me she had always wanted to call me for the money but had misplaced my contact information. She gave me the money there, and I counted it an eleventh-hour provision like in the time of Abraham at Mount Mariah, when he planned to sacrifice his only Son, but God provided.

Never give up. Our God provides when we think the future is full of darkness. As mentioned earlier, God is looking for an available, willing, and yielded vessel to use, and He will provide the tools needed. The tools can just be there without the user. Avail yourself for His service, and He will bring you the tools needed for His glory. Inner fears will be fought courageously when we know the tools will be provided.

When we live a life governed by faith, inner fear won't find a place in us because with faith, we know where to take our needs and problems. We don't get depressed by situations since we know the answer man, Jesus. Many times people waste time on anxiety, speculating on problems, but the word warns us against this. "Be careful for nothing; but in everything by prayers and supplications with thanksgiving, let your request be made known to God. And the peace of God that passeth all understanding shall keep your hearts and mind through Christ Jesus" (Philippians 4:6–7). Obeying these words overcomes inner fear because we are being reminded of what to do instead of wasting our precious time, which we could have used in service to God without unfruitful fretting. Peace that passes all understanding is well able to rid us of inner frets, and this is our promise from our dear, loving heavenly father.

Depressant medicines are very expensive, and such money could be used for the expansion of the body of Christ through evangelism if the word of God is applied rightly to overcome inner fear, which causes depression. With faith you can attain all your needs, and with the same, you cannot be intimidated by hassles that end up as inner frets. Going to Jesus takes our boldness amid many opposing powers, but the results are rewarding because they cancel every symptom that brings inner fear. In overcoming fear, we must accept that we are in a battle and should fight it rightly by faith to be conquerors. Fighting by flesh will bring only drastic defeat.

"For though we walk in the flesh, we don't war after the flesh, for the weapons of our warfare are not carnal but mighty through God to the pulling down of strongholds. Casting down imaginations and every high thing that exalteth itself against the knowledge of God and bringing into captivity every thought to the obedience of Christ; and having in readiness to revering all disobedience, when your obedience is fulfilled" (2 Corinthians 5:3–6). We are in the flesh, but our battle is spiritual and therefore requires spiritual armor of God. Our battle will be good if we win, and the word of God expects us by all means to be winners. For us to win, we must meet the laid-down conditions. Since the weapons aren't carnal, we need to draw spiritual power through serious prayers, fasting, and reading of the word. The strength of our food cannot fight a spiritual battle.

Many people speculate that they can be fully equipped for this battle by listening to the word of God only on Sundays. No way! One of the wicked sins of the body of Christ today is lack of the word. You must be eager to sit at the table of God and have the word the same way you sit to dine and have fun. Recreation time must be minimized, and the word must be fully covered in our programs if any success of overcoming fear is expected. We must know that the devil is very happy with those who are only Sunday goers because they are his prey, on whom he piles all kinds of inner fear. Eve was defeated in the Garden of Eden because she didn't have a word to tell the devil when he came before her, unlike Jesus who bombarded the devil's threats with "It is written." Without the word, you can't be a threat to the devil. A Sunday-only word isn't of God. Getting the Bible once a week is like one meal once a week. The way your body fails due to a lack of food is the same way the Spirit fails due to lack of the word. Man shall not live on bread alone. Why are we subtracting some scriptures to suit our laziness? Remember the warning in Revelation 22:18–19. "If ye abide in me and my words abide in you, ye shall ask what ye will and it shall be done" (John 15:7). You can't add to the word of God, nor can you subtract from it.

Have you missed something from God? Is His word abiding in you? Are you reminding Him of His promises to you in His word? On Friday evening, my son got a severe fever, and the following day, I was going for a mission for two days. My conscience alerted me that this was the devil's trap for me to reason things out realistically and hence fail to go on that mission. I ignored all the realities and reminded God of His promises as I laid my hands on my son. I reminded God that He had given me the burden of His work, and hence He intervened in that situation, and we slept. The following day, my son woke up very early and knocked on our bedroom door, testifying that he had been healed. My kids know that it's Jesus who heals, and before I pray for them, I normally ask them that question on which I also request God to honor their faith in them. Transparency before God helps to overcome inner fears. Hezekiah was able to overcome the obstacle that lay before him and the Israelites when he received that letter from Sennacherib, the king of Assyria.

> And Hezekiah received the letter from the hand of the messengers and read it, and Hezekiah went up unto the house of the lord, and spread it before the lord. And Hezekiah prayed unto the lord saying, O Lord of hosts, God of Israel that dwelleth between the cherubim's, thou art the God, even thou alone of all the kingdom's of the earth: thou hast made heaven and earth. Incline thy ear, O lord and hear; open thine eyes, o lord and see, and hear all the words of Senachrib which hath sent to reproach the living God, of a truth, Lord the kings of Assyria have laid waste all the nations and their countries, and have cast their gods into the fire: for they were not gods but the work of men's hands, wood and stone, therefore they have destroyed them. Now therefore, o lord our God, save us from his hand, that all the kingdoms of

## Fear Not; God Is in Charge

the earth may know that thou art the lord, even thou alone. (Isaiah 37:14–20)

Sennacherib's letter from the king of Assyria had bad contents, which caused fear, but this servant of God took a good action. Many times we receive bad news, but we fail to take the right action the way Hezekiah did.

This king was strong and was determined to deal nefariously with God's people, but when the right action was taken, he came under their feet. Our enemies will always be under our feet when we take the right action spiritually. The sequences of the steps Hezekiah took are worth being considered and applied in our lives, which are surrounded by threatening environments:

- He read the note.
- It went up to God's house.
- He spread it before the Lord.
- He prayed unto the Lord.

He read the note: Hezekiah wasn't ignorant the way some of us are. He took time to read that bad letter. We also need to take time to detail our bad situations in life before going to the house of the Lord, having read the details. He well knew the bad contents, and hence he was well conversant with what to tell God. We need to know specifically what we require from the Lord.

He went up to God's house: Having known well the dangers that had begotten him and his people, he went to God's house. He went to the right place to take his problems. God's house is the right place to take our needs and problems. Many are substituting God's house with bars to take one for the road. They are turning to witchcraft by going to consult the witch doctors, but I tell you these are just gods, which are the works of men's hands. They are temporal, and their results are regrets and waste of both money and time. Discover now the right place to take your problems like Hezekiah, and all will be well with you.

He spread it before the Lord: Hezekiah knew the secret of attaining anything from God was transparency. He never tried to go around the corner, but he struck the nail right on the head. He opened up before God and gave the entire burden he had. The letter was his burden. He laid it open before God. The all-knowing God must have well known the letter even before it was dispatched to Hezekiah, but Hezekiah still spread it before Him.

God knows us by name, and every detail of our lives is clearly known by Him, but He requires us to be transparent by will before Him. He wills that we take to Him all our burdens to Him willingly as we acknowledge His mighty intervention in the same. We don't need to behave like con men before God. Be transparent before God in that need you have. If you are suffering from AIDS, don't just mention the symptoms of AIDS, but be open and tell Him the root cause of the symptoms. Fear not before God because whether you tell Him or not, He knows you even better than you know yourself. Transparency before God brings full deliverance.

Elisha's servant was also very open when his axe-head fell into the water. He showed his master where it had fallen. "But as one was felling a beam, the axe head fell into the water: and he cried and said, alas, master! For it was borrowed. And the man of God said where fell it? (2 Kings 5:5–7). He recovered his axe-head because he was transparent. Suppose he had feared. What could have happened? Immediately the axe fell; he could have feared to tell the master lest others consider him careless, but I thank God for his boldness, and that caused the recovery of the axe-head, which had been borrowed.

Once you start seeing the future from a human perspective, you are doomed to fail, but once you look at it from the spiritual perspective, success will be sure. What will other people say is another tool the enemy is using to keep Christians down? Come on, friend. Mind what God says about you, and you will be more that a conqueror, because He will always encourage you with a "Fear not. You are mine." This story is very similar to the other one about Hezekiah, because when he sensed danger,

## Fear Not; God Is in Charge

- He cried.
- He showed the master the problem.

Now start being transparent instead of dodging God with your life. Show Him the problem, and He is always at your service. He will come when you call Him. When did you lose your heavenly vision? Be open to God, and because He is merciful, He will forgive you and restore you again for His use. When did you stop tithing, and what caused this? Be transparent before God, and He will be faithful to forgive you. It's never too late with God. You can start over again because He isn't a man to keep your old record of sins. He will forgive and forget, unlike mankind.

He prayed unto the Lord: Prayer was the final step of all the steps Hezekiah took, and it ended up well. The sequence of yours may be different, but they are all involved when we are marching right to heaven with the same compass, the word. When he prayed, God answered and encouraged him. If you pray, God will also answer you because He changes not. Runners never give up in the middle of the race, but they set their goals to reach the mark set for them to be considered winners. Hezekiah never gave up at step one, two, or three; but he accomplished all. We must be determined to accomplish all the steps to attain our God-set goals. Our flesh may weaken when we are in step two or three, but we must take courage the more, even as we know the spirit is always willing, but the flesh is weak. We must oppress our carnal body to lift the spiritual because we are fighting spiritual battles. We must be ready to deny our carnal body many things for the spiritual one to gain, but we shall not regret whatsoever. As we wait on the lord, we should never give up after trying only once.

David, who always sought the Lord again and again, found the right way. "Therefore David inquired of the lord saying; shall I go and smite these philistines? And the Lord said unto David, go and smite the philistines and save Keilah ... then David inquired of the lord yet again. And the lord answered him and said, arise, go down to Keilah; for I will deliver the philistines into thine hand ... and David abode in the wilderness in the strongholds, and remained in a mountain in the wilderness of Zip. And Saul sought him every day but God delivered him not into his hand" (1 Samuel 23:2, 4, 14). David sought God, not man—not once but every time he encountered a problem, and God always answered him, giving him the best advice and protection against his enemy, Saul. "Yet again" shows his persistence in seeking the Lord. Be persistent, my friend, to seek the Lord, and you will always get the best advice for your situation. He had prayed to God before, yet he never reasoned on his previous prayers, but he needed more and more of God's guidance and assurance.

God is never tired of our prayers. He is always keen to listen to us as His children through Jesus. Never speculate that you are bothering God by praying many times. Praying without ceasing is the principle. Saul struggled to seek David, but God protected him. Why? David always sought God for every burden. "But God delivered him not into his hands." The devil will struggle to pin you down by every available means to him, but be assured that as you always seek the Lord in prayers, God won't deliver you to the traps of the enemy. To summarize this chapter on overcoming inner fear, we must be determined to involve God, and He will honor our trust in Him.

# Chapter 10

# The Best Way to Deal with Fear

THE BEST WAY to deal with fear is to take the word of God in its real meaning without entertaining any doubts. Every time, fear not biblically should be tackled in a biblical way with all sincerity and obedience, since God's promises are yea and amen; then we should entirely depend on them to deal with fear the way He expects us to. Nevertheless, God's promises always have conditions attached to them, which must be met to attain victory over fear.

We must keep in mind that fighting fear is a call for us to obey what the word says, and as we combine all with prayers, we will be confident to say, "The Lord is my light and my salvation; whom shall I fear?" (Psalm 27:1). We need to be confident that we are well able to overcome fear in this race. We need to ignore every discouraging report by the enemy and his agents. We should be courageous like Caleb, who had another spirit.

"And Moses sent them to spy out the land of Canaan; and said unto them, get you up this way southward, and go up into the mountain: and see the land, what it is; and the people that dwelleth therein, whether they be strong or weak, few or many. And what the land is that they dwell in, whether in tents or in strongholds; and what the land is whether it be fat or lean, whether there be wood therein or not, and be ye of good courage, and bring the fruits of the land" (Numbers 13:17–20).

God had spoken to Moses, instructing him to send people to spy out their Promised Land, and he knew all there was. Moses never sent mere men, but all those he sent were the leaders of every tribe of Israel. Despite them being leaders, they all feared except Caleb. They all testified of the goodness of the land and even brought fruit samples. Nevertheless, a certain word gave them a thunderous defeat. The word they used was *dangerous*, which isn't of faith. Out of the twelve people, only one person, Caleb, brought an encouraging report without fear. God never works with multitudes or the-majority-wins principle. It isn't a spiritual language because if it was, they could have won.

Their first response to go was good, but their result was a total failure. In the spiritual realm, the end determines eternity. Embarking on our Christian life isn't enough. Running the distance amid various obstacles and crossing the finish line are what matters most. These twelve elders started off well, but what they saw in that land with their normal eyes discouraged their spiritual race. They forgot that God had promised them victory and that He never promises what He cannot fulfill. Were it not that they entertained fear, God wouldn't have left them without a means of guidance.

"And Caleb stilled the people before Moses and said, let us go up at once, and possess it for we are well able to overcome it" (v. 30). He alone knew that with God, they were able. He encouraged them. You and I have a responsibility to encourage the majority of our colleagues who, like Caleb, are giving up on the way. Caleb's stand with God was what made the difference. Our stand with God should make us encourage the discouraged lot. Individuality is what matters before God. Caleb looked to God and not to the people around him.

Many times, I have heard people say they can't get saved because of what they have seen saved people do while claiming to be better off than they are. My friend, the word says pointblank, "Looking unto Jesus, the author and the finisher of your faith." Don't look at people. If Caleb had looked at his fellow elders, he could have feared with

## Fear Not; God Is in Charge

them. If you look at people, your final destiny will be hell; but if you look at Jesus, heaven will be your rewarding destiny. Be encouraged now because the battle isn't yours, but God will fight for you.

Knowing our position in the light of the word will make us deal with fears effectively. God will testify of our stand in Him if we faint not, just the way He testified of Caleb. "But my servant Caleb, because he had another spirit with him and hath followed me fully, him will I bring into the land where into he went, and his seed shall possess it" (Numbers 14:24). If he had inner fear, he could have just followed the Lord like the others, but now that he didn't fear, he was able to follow God fully and individually at the measure of his personal faith in God.

May God help us to follow Him fully as we look to Him alone like this Caleb. Our following God fully will make us reach home, heaven, which He promised us when we trusted Him through His Son, Jesus Christ. Our children will also be partakers with us in heaven, even as the word encourages us that salvation is ours and even of our household. Caleb's children vowed they would possess that land just because of the faithfulness of their father. The "like father like son" saying proves to us that the determined spirit in Caleb was also in his children as they imitated his ways. When we follow God fully, our kids will imitate us and desire to live for the Lord from their tender age.

The land God had promised the Israelites was already inhabited, and He knew they needed to conquer it. Since God had promised, He was to give them the strength needed to conquer it. Whenever He promises us something—it doesn't matter who has it—it's ours once He says so. When He wants us to conquer it, He will always give us the ability, which is sure against all opposing powers. Caleb was confident of this fact, and no wonder he was able to say, "We are well able."

The devil and his angels already occupied our dwelling here on earth, yet God expected us to live here. This calls our attention to the fact that spiritual warfare is real, but we should fight a good fight and be confident that we are on the winning side with the Lord. Amen. That is a better way to deal with inner fear by focusing our whole being on success because of the Lord.

Dealing with fear from the Biblical perspective calls us to take the word of God as our mirror. A mirror helps us to work on a particular mistake, such as applying oil nicely to our faces, combing our hair uniformly, and so forth. The word of God in the same manner helps us to rectify our mistakes in this heavenly journey. In the area of immorality, it cautions us that without holiness, we cannot see God. For success, we need to meditate on the word day and night the Joshua way when he was taking over the leadership of the Israelites from Moses. We need the word to make us bold enough to testify of God's doings wherever we are. All in all, it is in the word. Our lives will be well shaped by this word, and as we soak ourselves in it completely, we will attain a powerful weapon against the devil's attempts to drive wedges in our mortal bodies. It's this word that will make us realize we have a God-given responsibility in these last days to increase the population of heaven while depopulating the devil's kingdom as we engage in evangelism because God's economy has no problem whatsoever.

A continuous anointing of the Lord in our daily lives is vital if we are to deal with inner fear effectively. Just as outside anointing dries off, the inside anointing can also dry off if we don't look into it carefully. When we get saved, the blood of Jesus cleanses us, and God counts us as one of His own. Retaining this anointing call for much effort by having a full spiritually balanced diet, with full nutrients contained in the word. Also like the way a vehicle battery needs recharging, we Christians need spiritual recharging from time to time to be effective on this heavenly journey.

Jesus, the Son of God, was anointed when the Holy Spirit filled Him. We also need the same as imitators of Christ (Luke 4:18–19).

Why do we need the anointing? The three things Jesus did after the anointing are preaching the good news to the poor, healing the broken hearted, and preaching deliverance to the captives. For us to have a heart for people like Jesus did, we need this anointing. With the daily anointing, no sin will be near us. In this world, we need to be anointed more than ever before if we expect any victory, because the devil is on a twenty-four-hour service to see us get down spiritually.

## Fear Not; God Is in Charge

The word will help us to be anointed as we obey God from Genesis to Revelation.

Well-fed children are always healthy, and they aren't prone to most health hazards. In the same way, a well-fed Christian with the word is always resistant to the attacks of the enemy. Do you want to be healthy spiritually? Start feeding on the word and you will see the outcome that will benefit both you and those you relate to. A poorly fed child suffers from malnutrition, which is a threat to his or her parents, society, and the nation because of the economy interference with medicines and relief food supply.

Spiritual malnutrition victims are also a threat to their own destiny and others too because they fail to take their responsibilities seriously. How? Lacking the word makes you a gossiper, someone who affects other people. You become a thief since you don't know the word that says, "Don't steal." You become an adulterer as you fail to realize that no adulterer will inherit the kingdom of God and hence affect other peaceful marriages. You fail to be an intercessor, and then peace fails in the country, causing a halt to the spread of the gospel of the kingdom of God effectively. You become lazy and forget that lazybones shouldn't even eat since everyone is supposed to eat of his or her own sweat since the fall of mankind in the Garden of Eden.

Suckers in coffee plants prevent good and healthy coffee berries, and the farmer spends time pruning the suckers because he knows the benefits; and in the same way, fear may cause our spiritual growth, as expected by our maker, to be retarded. We also need the word of God to prune us to reach God's expected standard. We need to take time to read it if any growth is to come. After the farmer prunes the suckers, he doesn't stop there; he proceeds to spray the coffee and even applies manure to enrich the fruits, which he will appreciate when the boom time comes.

Our boom time is when the Lord Jesus will come to earth. We need to meet all the costs of dealing with fear by applying spiritual manure, which is the word of God. We need to spray our lives with it, and the fruits of our lives will be worthy when He comes, and He will commend us with, "Well done, faithful servant, enter into the rest well prepared for you." Oh, what a joy that will be when we receive our reward! How I long for that time, and I hope you do also.

We shall forget the heartache we had while we spent many hours in praying, reading the word, preaching the gospel, and encouraging the discouraged lot; and the Lord will televise all the work we did on earth for all to see. Woe unto them that were just mere Christians and churchgoers with no other desire to do as the Lord desires. Besides them, there will be no decorations in their crowns, but it will be too late for them to do anything. If there is anything you should do, do it now, for the Lord is coming soon, and you'll deal with fear wisely in the wisdom of our God.

Realize we have a name, even as we do all sorts of things. This name is Jesus, and it is very valuable to us. This Jesus charms our fears, cancels eternal damnation. and paves the way for a better end. It is the best aspect, even in heaven. It's this name we call on, and we are saved. "For whosoever will call upon the name of the Lord shall be saved" (Romans 10:13). *Whosoever* includes you if you aren't yet saved. Call on that name now and be saved. There are several captions on earth, but this name Jesus surpasses them all. It's this name when called on that cancels divorce and restores joy in marriages. Abiding in this name can make us the richest people on earth. "If ye abide in me, and my words abide in you, ye shall ask what ye will and it shall be done unto you" (John 15:17). *What ye want* is asking all you wish, but first meet the condition of abiding in Him and His words. For every promise of God, there are conditions to be met, and so the decision remains with you.

This name is so powerful that it empowers us to become the children of God. As you receive this name Jesus, you automatically become a child of God. Many tend to speculate that all mankind are God's children, but friend, let me assure you well that without Jesus, you are only a creation of God but not His child since the fall of mankind in the Garden of Eden. Before Adam and Eve sinned, we were in a good relationship with God, but when sin entered, we were subtracted from the initial perfect plan of God. Nevertheless, because God is so merciful, He sent His only-begotten Son, Jesus, so that as

## Fear Not; God Is in Charge

we accept Him as Lord and Savior, we get an additional factor toward the plan of God, thereby bringing a cross sign.

An additional factor from God for reconciling mankind to God and the end result if you join the two is a cross sign: +. Mankind minus Jesus makes us only a creation of God but not children. Add Jesus, and you become a child of God. Decide now your fate by choosing the Jesus. The word of God gives us the confidence to know our rights, and not until we read the word will we know these rights. You will know the truth, and the truth will set you free. You can be freed from the bondage of inferiority when you confidently know that the word says you are fearfully and wonderfully made in the image of God. Deal with fear effectively and wisely by having the word of God.

The word clearly states that through the stripes of Jesus, we are healed. The devil comes to uninformed Christians carrying a symptom of a particular disease, and he confronts you with a headache, leaving depression in the storehouse of all diseases. Failing to claim your right of healing, you just accept and even confess, "Once this headache of mine starts the next time, I will have sleepless nights for two good weeks." There you are, digging and nurturing the ground for the enemy to go back quickly, come with depression, and plant it in your well-fed soil, and you will be as you confessed. Come on! You have no disease of your own. You have only health as a child of God.

The devil is the father of all lies, and he wants to keep you sickly and hence prevent your service for God. If we all get sick, who will preach to the sick people? Who will till the land? Yet God expects us to eat the fruits of the works of our hands. Behave as Jesus did in the wilderness. When the devil came before Him, He just told him, "It is written." Tell him the same, and victory will be yours; you will have the peace of God that passes all human comprehension.

With the right word for a particular circumstance, you are already a winner. Just take your stand on the promises of God, and the devil will know you are a child of God. Once you overcome once, be well informed that the same devil never gives up on you. He will try another time. He did the same to Jesus three times, and the Bible records, "And when the devil had ended all the temptations, he departed from him for a season" (Luke 4:13).

Always, the devil departs for a time, not forever. This should keep us alert and in the word fully, occupying our minds because he is always looking for another time. At that other time, use that other word, which you read another time, and be able to deal with inner fear effectively. As he looks for that other time to bring another temptation, be busy looking for that other word, with which you will tell him again, "It is written."

As soldiers, we are to be ready for battle because when we confessed Christ as our Lord and Savior, we declared a warfare with the enemy. He uses different strategies, but with God, who has provided us with enough bullets to fight back this determined enemy, victory is ours but only when we make use of our spiritually designed weapons in the word of God combined with prayers. The greatest secret I have learned of the word of God is that it's just to the level of hearing. The most learned ones comprehend it the way the illiterate ones do; they have the same impact so long as it's taken in obedience.

I have seen many who have never gone to school receiving miracles from God just because of obeying and believing the preached word. This brings the spiritual equality that fits together people of different calibers. The almighty God, who isn't a respecter of persons, ministers to us the same way provided we obey. Simply applying it in our lives are the principles that bring success. The word makes us stable in the Lord, and hence we manage the many threats of life without being tossed to and fro, unlike the Galatians who made Paul wonder, "I marvel that ye are so soon removed from him that called you into the grace of Christ unto another gospel" (Galatians 1:6). These people weren't rich in the word of God because if they had been, they wouldn't have been removed from the original gospel of Christ, which they had heard. Such Christians are still there today who always move from one sect to another in search of new anointing, forgetting that the anointing will come upon them wherever they are so long as they obey the word and have it richly dwelling in them. That isn't managing fear well biblically.

## Fear Not; God Is in Charge

Stability shows Christian maturity because you desire to make others reach your level of spirituality instead of moving to another sect. Sects aren't the way, and the word clearly states the only way. Jesus is the way and the answer, and above Him there is no other. "Jesus saith unto him, I am the way, the truth and the life: no man cometh unto the father but by me" (John 14:6). If you haven't read these words, you cannot know that Jesus is the only way to heaven. Your moving from one sect to another will only add more problems as you find many Christians at fault as you roam like a nomadic Christian. Read the word well and hide it in your heart, and stability where you are will be sure.

Our costs of knowing our rights in God are reading, obeying, and applying the word to our respective needs. It's time we tell the devil that enough is enough of what he denied us for long because we have known our rights are in the word, which we have read and believed. These demands from the enemy aren't easily attained, but we have to get them violently. No wonder the word says that the kingdom of God suffers violence and that only the violent must take it by force. Soft language with the devil never works. You must attack him the Bible way by throwing at him all the available promises in the word.

He is a thief, and this is clearly stated; tell him pointblank about this. Once you expose a thief even in your town, he or she runs for his or her life. Expose this thief, Satan, who has stolen so many things in our lives, such as joy, peace, health, prosperity, and boldness as he partly quotes the Bible. His experience in stealing has made Him so daring that He always steals some word from the Bible to accomplish His ill motives against us.

He did the same to our Savior, Jesus. And he brought Him to Jerusalem, set Him on a pinnacle of the temple, and said to Him, "For it is written, he shall give his angels charge over thee, to keep and in their hands they shall bear thee up, lest at any time thou dash thy foot against a stone." So be on the alert because the devil also knows the scriptures, but he quotes only those verses that fit his strategy of getting you down spiritually.

In such a situation, you need to be very wise because if you are the type that gets the word only on Sundays without meditating on it fully on your own, you can easily be his prey. The devil is very keen on our daily lives, and he looks for a very suitable chance to hoodwink us.

At one end of the month, I was going to check my salary, and I counted and rechecked the first time and the second. There was an excess of four hundred shillings. For your information, my needs were more than the net salary I was getting at that time. There was a very suitable chance the devil wanted to use the excess on me, but praise be to God, I knew it wasn't a miracle from God, as many would term it. I am sure the devil created the surplus purposely to trap me. All the same, I once again glorify God and give honor to His holy name, because our God is ready to work on our clear consciences.

I returned the excess to the paying cashier, and he commented, "Imagine. I did not understand where the four hundred shillings went."

I replied in an evangelical way. "God allowed it to me specifically as a Christian so that He can teach me more about transparency and honesty." I repeated this twice to have the message sink into his mind well. All he said was "Asante" (thank you). What is that trap the devil is laying before you and confounding you to believe? He is always looking for that right time and chance. For example, in marriages, he times when you are angry, and then your spouse comes, demanding something from you in harsh language. In response, if you aren't keen with the word, you get trapped, and you answer back in a way that adds salt to an injury. The devil has overtaken you. Be keen in the word, and he will never overtake you.

In the Garden of Eden, he looked for the right time after God had forbidden them not to eat of that tree in the middle of the garden. He posed well before Eve: "Did God say to you that you don't eat of this tree?" Take care lest you be humbugged because that is his full-time job. Eve had no word from God that she could hold on and tell the devil, "It is written." Do you have a word to hold on to when he comes to you through that chance he is eagerly waiting for? If you don't, please start studying the word of God seriously to show

## Fear Not; God Is in Charge

yourself approved as His servant, who need not be ashamed. Hiding God's word in your heart is the only way to keep the devil away once he shows up. David, a man after God's own heart, knew this secret when he said, "I've hidden the word of God in my heart that I may not sin against him." There is a shortcut to overcoming the enemy and ruler of this world, Satan; we must have the word, which is the sword. By the way, be informed that the devil knows the word but with the wrong motive—to mislead the saints. He uses the word in a cunning way, so we surely need to know the word fully. Be filled with the spirit of discernment and full of courage as soldiers in the battlefield. Our hearts are like banks, which we use to deposit money to use in time of need, but if you don't deposit money, you cannot withdraw anything, no matter how desperate you may be. Regular deposits to your bank account determine how much you can benefit when a financial need arises. Daily and regular study of God's word and meditation will determine how you handle any need or challenge you encounter. There is a word for everything under the sun, be it good, bad, or encouraging—whatever term you encounter. In joy, you can rejoice; in sorrow, you find comfort; in loneliness you realize there is one who sticks closer than a brother (Proverbs 18:24). In sickness, He was chastened for our sins, by whose stripes we are healed (Isaiah 53:5).

As you travel to and from places, you get assurance of His presence and protection (Psalm 121). He will be with you as you go out and come in. All year-round guidance gives you peace of mind as long as you have the right word deposited in your heart for the right moment and challenge. Like a bullet aimed at the enemy in the battlefield, so is the word of God rightly used that gives you victory for every circumstance. A question may rise right now in your mind. Why then do Christians get discouraged if they have all these assurances? Good question, and the answer will be as normal as can be. Let's say you go to the bank and put in the PIN number you have always used in the past, but it fails to work. What do you do? I guess you try again, and if that doesn't work, you don't give up if you really need that money. If the bank is open, you go inside to a teller, or you call the customer service number. "Quitters never win, and winners never quit" is the strategy here.

Your need determines your persistence. Remember the woman and the rich man? Her need was beyond any challenge or ignorance; she never gave up until the rich man said, "Though I never fear God or respect anyone, I will grant this woman her need so she will stop bothering me at night." It was night, but her need was beyond reasoning in terms of daytime or nighttime. In dire need, you will keep knocking on heaven's door until it opens for you. Use every word you have in your heart account respectively, and you will get a response, but remember, a no from God is as good as a yes, though as human beings we tend to think that only when we get a yes is it right. We need to realize that "God's will" in whatever we ask is the key to our spiritual breakthrough. Jesus at Gethsemane had desired the cup of pain be removed, and after some time of calling on God, He said, "Nevertheless, your will be done."

What is it that you are going through? Are you expecting a yes? I bet. What if the painful situation persists? Get a word of comfort, and the Holy Spirit who work like a computer operator will press the reminding button for you, and you will hear a comforting word at a distance or in stillness: "My grace is sufficient." Despite the pain, the grace of God will be enough just like Paul and the thorn in the flesh. Paul prayed not once but several times before the word *grace*. How many times or for how long have you been pleading for that hard situation you've been going through? May the Holy Spirit quicken you to remember that our equation of timing in our human perspective is completely different from God's. One day is like a thousand years, and a thousand years are like a day before God. What you speculate has been like a thousand years of suffering could be just a day before God, but praise His holy name, because He never leave us without help, His grace.

What is grace? It's unmerited favor. Amen! It's what you don't deserve but was availed for you at your time of need. Before God's grace is embraced in our lives, nothing seems to be fair in our eyes, but in God's eyes, everything is under control as He promised not to let

## Fear Not; God Is in Charge

us be tempted beyond our ability. When you think you are at the end of everything and hopeless, that's just the beginning of God. Many faithful servants of God feel the same way, and we can always identify with a similar character in God's word. Elijah said, "I'm the only one left," and he was sorry for his life. He had given up as a human being because the situation was hard at that time, when he said, "I have had enough" (a statement of desperation in a dead-end situation).

God showed up and told him, "Arise, for the journey is long." He was strengthened (1 Kings 19). In your hour of desperation, be assured that God will show up and intervene on your behalf. Amen! God has many ways to get us out of any mess, disappointment, or depressing condition. Yes, and now you might be wondering and saying in your heart, *If only this woman knows what I'm going through.* And sure enough, I cannot know how you feel and what you are going through, but God, maker of heaven and earth, knows you, your feelings, and your disappointments. He is in total control of it all. He is Emmanuel, God with us, God with you now. Hallelujah to the Lamb of God, who reconciled us back to God when we were deeply lost in sins and separated from our heavenly Father, Jesus Christ, our mediator who came to give us hope beyond unbearable conditions.

Like in the case of Elijah, God is in the business of assigning angels tasks to attend us at our hour of desperation and real need. The angels will use divine means to deliver us from those hard situations as only God can do. Elijah had a ready-to-eat cake and water not from a regular bakery; it was baked by angels. Whatever ingredients used were good enough to overcome both physical and spiritual hunger for Elijah.

Whenever God intervenes, you can never be the same anymore. Your situation becomes an encouragement to many generations, even as you still get encouraged by this situation Elijah was in, and no wonder the word of God needs to be transferred from the book, the Bible, to our hearts for a day of encouragement. Your today's desperation can be someone else's inspiration and encouragement, but you must share it. Don't just keep it to yourself, for we are all parts of the same body of Christ. Be like a river that is always flowing with water, with a supply that never runs out. The more you share the story of encouragement while glorifying God, the more revelation will come through the Holy Spirit so the body of Christ can be edified as the days of getting to meet Him draw near.

Fear not as you share the story of deliverance and victory though you may be misunderstood and thought to be bragging. That's normal in this pilgrim's journey; if the world talked of Jesus, who are you to be exceptional? As His follower, you expect to experience little of what He did too. Personally, I've been misunderstood whenever I testify of God's victory, and people say I'm showing off, but I'm so happy; the word encourages me that if I should boast, it should be because of Christ. Amen. You can be thought of as being judgmental or self-righteous, but as long as you know your motives are right, keep on, and in the long run, the Savior will tell you, "Well done" after all is said and down. Never give up, for quitters never win, and winners never quit. Always be focused on the Savior, the author and finisher of your faith. We are like a city built on a hill that cannot be hidden, and all we do and say matters both before God and before those who see and hear us. We are ambassadors representing God; we are a walking, living Bible that needs to be read well by those who never have time to read it or go to church.

At one's home or place of work, as you drive on those highways where selfishness is the norm, overtaking without signaling a basic traffic requirement, texting while driving though forbidden by law, can one look at you and me and say we are unique? How well are you legible as a living, walking Bible? We all have our shortcomings, and our God is a God of second chances, which is heaven's heart policy. You can start afresh; all you need to do is confess in sincerity, and as a loving and forgiving heavenly Father, He will embrace you with love like you have never misbehaved before. Like the prodigal son when he regained his consciousness and took a step, you will experience tremendous joy in the Savior's loving hug, full of forgiveness.

What is that situation you are going through that scares you beyond your ability? Can you let God take charge because He not only is able but also will help you go through it with peace and courage?

## Fear Not; God Is in Charge

I must say this book has been like a prophecy in my own life, which is always faced with things that make me fret as a human; but once I handle it in the light of God's word, fear fades. So I wrote to encourage not only readers but also myself. Some of my working colleagues may testify of these reasons, especially those I have had a burden to mentor in this journey by encouraging, challenging, and giving a shoulder to lean on during my fears.

In this journey, there is no giant, but we are all prone to fear at some point in life, and no wonder there are the words "Fear Not." Great men of God have fear in their lives, but once the Lion of Judah (Jesus Christ, Son of the most high God) is involved, He drives away all fear. Amen. Don't be too hard on yourself, thinking you are a nobody because you always fear. Cheer up; you aren't alone. We are all humans and not angels; thus we give angels work to minister to us when we are overtaken by fear due to the commission of our God.

# About The Author

THE AUTHOR OF "Fear Not, God Is In charge, Pastor Florence Maina understands the realities of this life that make every person fear at some point in life for various reason. She points every fear you as a reader might have faced or will face in the future as an avenue to point you to God through His holy word in the bible to overcome fear. Not by your own strength but by the powerful spoken word of God which is readily available as long as you are willing to read it and believe that God is faithful to fulfil what He has promised

**Credentials:**

Professionally, Pastor Florence Maina is a Certified Medical Assistant and work full time with North Memorial Health, Minnesota, USA, a job she loves and have been with the organization over the past twelve years.

In ministry, Pastor Florence Maina has the following achievements which equip her better for her passion of serving the Lord:

1. Certified Stephen Minister, awarded by Stephen Ministries, St. Louis, USA. Trained through her local home church Grace Fellowship, Brooklyn Park, MN where she has been actively serving in the care ministry under the leadership of pastor John Cordova.
2. Ordained Pastor through International Outreach Church, Burnsville, Minnesota, USA under the leadership of Dr. Charles Karuku who is her spiritual mentor in ministry.

3. Trained Safe Journey program Volunteer Advocate through North Memorial Health, Minnesota, USA since March, 2013
4. Certified in Dealing with Difficult People through Fred Pryor Seminars, a division of PARK University Enterprises Inc., USA
5. Certified in Communication Skills for Women through Fred Pryor Seminars, a division of PARK University Enterprises Inc., USA

Pastor Florence is a gospel music composer, writer and singer. She has four Albums recorded most of which are in different languages: Kikuyu, Kiswahili and English as she clearly understands the "World Vision Protocol".

**Awards:**

**August,2016** – Appreciation award as The Guest of Honor by World Interfaith & Peace Harmony Summit in conjunction with ILM 2016, Chennai, India

**September,2017** – Appreciation award by Queens Night Ministry, Minnesota under the leadership of Pastor Laura Githinji of JCC, Twin Cities for continued community services.

**October,2018** - "Golden Award" 2$^{nd}$ position in one of her songs: "NJARAMIRIA MIHAKA" as Female Praise Song of the year 2018, Diaspora Region by One Word Miracle Radio, Seattle, Washington

**October,2018** – "Golden Award" 1$^{st}$ position as the Best Female Presenter of the year "Celebrate Your Moment with Joy", Diaspora Region by One Word Miracle Radio International, Seattle, Washington

**October,2018** – African Traditional Song of the Year "NJARAMIRIA MIHAKA" by GSMTV Network, Minnesota

She is the founder of "Celebrate Your Moment with Joy", a media ministry through which she minister daily video devotionals to many people all over the world as long as one has access to the radio, YouTube, Facebook and other media avenues.